How to Avoid Strangers on Airplanes is a sharp and witty exploration of the quirks of frequent flying, blending humor and insight with practical lessons for life and career. Drawing on his experience as both a seasoned road warrior and M&A executive, Brandon C. Blewett offers a hilariously relatable take on the habits of fellow travelers, transforming the chaos of air travel into a masterclass on navigating personal and professional growth. For frequent flyers and ambitious professionals who've ever sighed at the antics of gate lice or overhead bin battles, this is an indispensable read.

Gary Leff | Founder, View from the Wing and Co-Founder, InsideFlyer.com

Brandon Blewett's *How to Avoid Strangers on Airplanes* is a must-read for anyone who's ever navigated the consulting grind, survived the professional services hustle, or sprinted through an airport while questioning their life choices. It's packed with laughs and moments of catharsis that are painfully real for those of us who've lived it. Beyond the humor, Brandon's stories remind us how those shared experiences—no matter how absurd—shape the leadership skills and grit that amplify our careers.

Drew Chambers | Private Equity Investor, Entrepreneur, and Consulting and Investment Banking Veteran

I didn't expect a book about annoying airplane habits to teach me so much about leadership, but that's exactly what *How to Avoid Strangers on Airplanes* does. It is brilliantly witty and insightful. I am one of those who loves airplane food and gets excited about transiting through new airports! I got relate to the references of 'the gate lice' and 'the window wobbler' as I have been known to do that myself. But hopefully not on a flight with Brandon!

Dr. Deepak Bhootra | CEO, Jabulani Consulting, Houston, USA

Brandon Blewett's *How to Avoid Strangers on Airplanes* is a hilarious and refreshingly honest take on navigating travel, career pivots, and the chaos of professional life. As someone who's spent years flying between continents and reinventing my career, I found this book not just entertaining but deeply relatable. It's a must-read for anyone who's ever questioned their next move at cruising altitude—or in life.

Luke Milton | Entrepreneur and Founder, Training Mate, Revenge Body trainer, Former professional rugby player

As a frequent business traveler, I found Brandon Blewett's sharp wit and keen insights incredibly relatable. *How to Avoid Strangers on Airplanes* is a perfect blend of humor and career advice, making those long-haul flights a little less painful. I'm applying his leadership lessons both in the air and on the ground.

Glenn Hopper | Author, AI *Mastery for Finance Professionals*

As someone who travels frequently for work, I found *How to Avoid Strangers on Airplanes* to be funny and amazingly relatable. A platinum level expert on the dos and don'ts of traveling, Brandon relays his message using hilarious anecdotes that make you say "Been there!" More enjoyable, is the way he connects these episodes to the turbulence we encounter in our personal and professional lives. It's a reminder to keep going and to never settle for the middle seat.

Geoff Arnold | Baltimore Orioles Radio and Television Announcer.

Brandon Blewett's *How to Avoid Strangers on Airplanes* hilariously captures the chaos and quirks of frequent travel while sneaking in sharp reflections on navigating career and life. As entrepreneurs who know what it's like to live on the road, we found this book both cathartic and endlessly entertaining. A great read for anyone grinding toward their goals.

Zach Milewski and Hayden Cortez | Tech Entrepreneurs and Co-Hosts of the *Apps & Asphalt* Podcast

Blewett takes the pain out of frequent travel and turns it into hilarious, practical advice for managing both planes and people. A must-read for business travelers looking for a little levity and a lot of leadership wisdom.

Noelle Demole | Founder & CEO, Egidays

Raw, unapologetic, and refreshingly honest, *How to Avoid Strangers on Airplanes* is a good-natured, laugh-out-loud exploration of career and life's absurdities. Brandon doesn't take himself—or the corporate world—too seriously, which makes this book a joy to read. Whether you're just beginning your career journey or reflecting on your role as a leader, this book offers humor, insight, and a much-needed break from the usual self-help fare. A must-read for anyone who's ever stepped foot in an airport—or an office.

Joseph M. Mack | Ole Miss MBA Board President and Healthcare System Executive

HOW TO AVOID STRANGERS ON AIRPLANES:

SURVIVAL GUIDE FOR
THE FREQUENT BUSINESS TRAVELER

Bill,

From one road warrior to another, here's some humor to lighten the chaos. If this book brings even a fraction of the wit and insight that yours did, I'll consider it a success.

Cheers!

BRANDON C. BLEWETT

ISBN:

ISBN: 979-8-33962-632-9 (pbk)

ISBN: 979-8-33962-646-6 (hcv)

Library of Congress Control Number (LCCN): 2024920136

About the Author

Brandon Blewett holds "Million Miler" status with one U.S. airline and currently enjoys top-tier status with two of the largest U.S. carriers. His secret? An endless parade of work travel that would make even a nomad blush. Brandon often jokes that his permanent residence is simply where he pays property taxes, as he seems to actually live in the sky, on planes, or in airports.

Brandon currently leads the M&A engine at a private equity-backed paving company as the head of corporate development. Each week, he travels to visit potential acquisition targets or recently acquired businesses, ensuring smooth transitions as they integrate into the platform. This role is the result of fourteen years of global deal experience, encompassing more than $210 billion in transaction value. Before paving the way (pun absolutely intended), he directed corporate strategy and development for a building products company, thanks to his time in professional services.

Brandon sharpened his transaction skills in the whirlwind world of management consulting. He worked at two of the world's largest consulting and advisory firms. Starting in M&A tax and transitioning to M&A strategy, he spent over a decade in professional services during a time when consulting still demanded weekly travel—departing on Mondays and returning on Thursdays. This routine provided a front-row seat to the often peculiar and perturbing habits of travelers on planes and in airports. Through this journey, Brandon discovered the joys, pain points, and ultimate hacks of a career in professional services, learning that the tumultuous trip from departure to destination closely mirrors the way we navigate our career journeys.

The experiences and insights in this book have been carefully curated and written by Brandon himself, drawing directly from his personal journey through the highs and lows of constant travel and navigating his professional journey.

Table of Contents

Preface

If you're reading this, chances are you've spent more time in airport terminals than you care to admit. You've probably mastered the art of packing in fifteen minutes flat, can recite the TSA guidelines in your sleep, and have a preferred aisle seat locked and loaded on every airline app. But even the most seasoned road warrior can't escape the inevitable encounters with fellow travelers who, for lack of a better term, test your patience at 30,000 feet.

This book was born out of my own frequent flyer frustrations. What started as a series of mental notes to cope with the quirks and idiosyncrasies of air travel evolved into this guide—a snarky, yet hopefully insightful, companion for the weary business traveler. Over the years, I've had the (mis)fortune of observing a cast of characters who seem to make it their mission to turn a routine flight into an episode of *Survivor*. From the Gate Lice who swarm the boarding area like it's a Black Friday sale to the Conference Call Deci-bullies who think the entire airport needs to hear their quarterly earnings report, these habits are as predictable as they are annoying.

But this book isn't just about venting frustrations. It's about the lessons we can learn from these encounters—lessons that extend far beyond the airport. You see, in many ways, navigating the world of air travel is a lot like navigating the professional world. Both environments are high-stakes, fast-paced, and require a certain level of strategic thinking to succeed. The behaviors we observe in the airport often mirror those we encounter in the boardroom, the client pitch, or even the team meeting. By recognizing these parallels, we can turn every irritating travel experience into an opportunity for personal and professional growth.

In the following pages, you'll find a mix of humor, anecdotes, and practical advice, all framed through the lens of the six most annoying habits of travelers. Whether you're a consultant, investment banker, financier, lawyer, or just someone who's tired of the constant battle for overhead bin space, this book is for you. My goal is to not only make you laugh but also to provide a fresh perspective on how these small, seemingly insignificant moments in our travel lives can actually teach us something valuable.

So, as you embark on your next business trip, I invite you to keep this guide handy. After all, the next time you're seated next to a Backpack Wrecking Crew member or stuck behind an Eager Exiter, you might just find yourself reflecting on the broader lessons these encounters offer. And who knows? You might even start to see these annoyances as opportunities for growth rather than obstacles to endure.

Welcome aboard, and let's navigate this journey together—preferably from the comfort of an upgraded seat with extra legroom and complimentary champagne.

A Frequent Flyer's Disclaimer

The following tales come from the hectic life of a frequent flyer on the road, making deals and dodging travel nightmares. All observations are through the snarky lens of someone often sleep deprived with vision blurred from staring at a laptop screen. While the stories are based on actual events, some names and locations have been altered to protect the guilty and to avoid awkward encounters in airport lounges. Any resemblance readers draw to passengers they've encountered, whether living or catatonically inept, is purely coincidental and highly unfortunate. Unless, of course, you recognize yourself—then it's purely intentional.

Chapter 1

Welcome to the Terminal

Let me guess, you hate the airport. I take no offense. An odd follow-on sentence perhaps, but I jokingly refer to the airport as my "home" due to the countless hours I spend there each year for work travel. I take neither blame for the cuisine nor credit for the architecture. I actually sympathize with your disdain. Hell, sometimes I even feel it. We have a love-hate relationship. Air travel often brings out the worst in people. When it does, make no mistake—it's the absolute worst. It's road rage without the sound shield of a vehicle and the accompanying ability to flee the scene and avoid conflict. We laugh at memes or social media posts that showcase the highlight reels, but you and I are both guilty of thinking, speaking or acting in ways that would drive the most ardent atheist to a confessional booth. Airports comprise a mere microcosm of our daily world, yet they amplify minor stressors and irritants to irrational, macrocosmic levels. Why?

I opine that the largest driver of this magnification stems from the forced intermingling of complete strangers under pressure and in close proximity for prolonged periods of time. Merriam-Webster most commonly defines the word "stranger" as a noun and does so in less than rosy terms. Fact-checkers will find words like "intruder" or phrases such as "one who does not belong" and "one that interferes without right." Frustratingly, strangers – to the tune of thousands – line airport terminals like obstacles in a Super Mario Brothers game. We all view ourselves as the main character of the video game, whether it's Mario, Luigi, Peach, or Yoshi, and we see other passengers as the barriers, such as Goombas, Koopas, or Piranha Plants. But that viewpoint fails to consider that everyone is playing the same game from the same console at the same time. We're all trying to reach our destination without losing our sanity or our luggage. In doing so, we simply wish to avoid one another in the process. And thus, we must ask – is that possible? Can we avoid strangers on airplanes, at airports, and during air travel altogether?

As former President Obama frequently stated, "Let me be clear." This book makes no grand promises to change your next trip. It won't eliminate wait times at TSA or ensure first-class upgrades. It's not a science book of the physics or social varieties. Instead, we will underscore how our interactions with strangers during air travel mirror similar encounters along our professional journeys and the valuable lessons we can draw from each to help us navigate our own flight paths. Fear not; you won't read manifestation doctrines or receive discounts for the essential oils best suited to channel your creativity as you scan countless images to build your Pinterest vision board. No, no, that would be too easy— and accompanied by lavish speaking conferences and $25,000 "inner circles."

Jokes aside, our professional lives do mimic air travel, a journey replete with departures, connections, delays, turbulence, cancellations, and arrivals. In between these phases, people often find themselves in holding patterns, a seemingly endless loop on their career flights. But holding patterns don't signify a lack of success. After all, you're airborne. Still, that doesn't eliminate the frustration of limbo or a prolonged detour at an unplanned location. My hope is that the following pages will help identify the navigational beacons, approach paths, and runway lights to exit the holding pattern and navigate you toward an intended and desired destination. Hopefully, with some laughs along the way. Even if they are at my expense.

Two characters, Susan and Steve, help us begin our journey.

I'll Just Drive Myself

Susan glanced at the Uber app, only to discover a mind-boggling 3X surge. "$140? Are they out of their minds?" she exclaimed, refusing to fork over such a ludicrous amount. It was now clear that summoning an Uber was out of the question. Why pay extra when parking her own car on-site would save her $75? Susan double-checked the airport website, which confirmed parking availability. A quick check on Google Maps revealed an estimated travel time of 28 minutes. "Perfect!" she declared, feeling a surge of confidence as she hopped into her car, leaving with ample buffer time. Little did she know, the highway had other plans for her.

In a stroke of automotive drama, a Toyota Prius engaged in a gladiator-style showdown with a mighty Chevy Avalanche right before Susan's eyes. The vehicles proudly displayed bumper stickers supporting opposing causes and candidates, like political rivals battling it out on the asphalt battlefield. Susan couldn't help but chuckle as she envisioned their heated exchange. But as minutes turned into an eternity, her amusement morphed into frustration. Forty-five minutes trapped in traffic and still counting. Just when she thought things couldn't get worse, the sky unleashed a symphony of thunder and a downpour that rivaled a high-powered car wash. "Oh, perfect! Because apparently, the fine folks in this city needed another excuse to drive like total idiots today," Susan muttered, feeling her optimism slowly dissipate like a deflating tire. The knot in her stomach tightened with each passing minute, fearing that dreaded flight cancellation text from the airline. "No, no, no. Stay positive," she half-heartedly reassured herself, secretly hoping for a delay to match the severity of the traffic nightmare. The sight of planes taking off and landing in a synchronized dance offered a glimmer of hope that her flight to Philadelphia might still depart as scheduled. But deep down, Susan wondered, would she be on that plane?

Susan careened off the highway towards the airport with the fervor of a cheetah on a cocaine bender, determined to maintain her speed while dutifully adhering to the colossal signs and convoluted arrows that promised to guide her through the labyrinthine maze of concrete to the correct parking garage. Just when GPS was about to exclaim, "You've arrived," Susan abruptly slammed on the brakes, narrowly avoiding an army of five blindingly bright orange cones and an imposing detour sign. The detour left Google Maps utterly flabbergasted, and Susan could have sworn she detected a hint of annoyance in the typically polite, British voice she had chosen as her navigation companion. As if fate had a wicked sense of humor, Susan's cell service abruptly vanished, leaving her feeling vulnerable and stranded— *Naked and Afraid* airport edition.

Susan unleashed a fifteen-minute symphony of intermittent expletives, screams and prayers, channeling equal parts frustration and spiritual desperation. Finally, by some miracle, she stumbled upon a parking garage on the opposite side of the airport, offering a meager twenty-seven parking spots invisible to the human eye at the exorbitant rate of an extra $25 per day. "So much for any savings," she thought as she firmed her grip on the steering wheel. She finally found a parking spot on the top level, uncovered, just as the rain resumed. When Susan left her house, she envisioned a leisurely glass of Sauvignon Blanc before her flight—a tranquil prelude to her journey. Instead, she arrived at the terminal embodying two of Catherine O'Hara's unforgettable characters: Mrs. McAllister sprinting through Chicago O'Hare and Moira Rose experiencing an emotional breakdown when Interflix unceremoniously dumped *The Crows* movie. Today, with Phil Collins' *Against All Odds* at max volume in her ears, she would challenge her high school track days and record-setting speeds... in Tory Burch flats.

Your Uber Has Arrived

Steve was convinced that his airport routine was foolproof. He had become a seasoned traveler, relying on his faithful driver, Sammy, for his weekly commutes. Sammy, the mastermind behind a fleet of five vehicles and drivers, always made sure to chauffeur Steve personally. With an encyclopedic knowledge of traffic shortcuts and insider tips on the airport's hidden drop-off and pick-up spots, Sammy was the epitome of a transportation virtuoso. He utilized apps like FlightAware to track Steve's flights and traffic-monitoring apps to stay ahead of highway congestion and give Steve a heads-up if a timely pick-up adjustment was needed. And let's not forget those rare occasions when Steve overindulged the night before – Sammy had the distinguished honor of access to Steve's keypad lock to unleash an onslaught of relentless knocking until Steve awoke and readied himself for departure. In fairness, that only happened seven times in six years—thanks, Casamigos. During their rides, they covered everything from world affairs to personal matters, making the journey feel like a friendly catch-up session. Steve never had to worry about missing a flight or fret over delays. Until today. Unfortunately, fate had a different plan for Steve as he prepared to head to Philadelphia. Sammy had to cancel at the last minute due to a family emergency. Steve expressed genuine empathy via text, sent a generous $250 gift card to the family, and reluctantly booked an Uber Black that would undoubtedly raise eyebrows when he filed his expense report the following week. Although it meant a fifteen-minute setback to secure a ride, Steve was confident he could still arrive at the airport without dampening his newest Mizzen + Main button-down. Oh, how wrong he was. Very, very wrong.

In a grand display of lane-choice incompetence, Steve's driver proudly avoided the glorious HOV lane, where cars zoomed along at or above the speed limit, while the other lanes resembled the agonizing crawl of a snail marathon. To add insult to injury, the driver clung to the rightmost lane, serving as a makeshift parking lot as cars hopped on and off the highway from every imaginable ramp. Desperately attempting to keep his cool, Steve valiantly tried to focus on the chaotic Zoom call blaring through his earbuds. Squinting like a detective deciphering a cryptic message, he strained his eyes to read the microscopic slides on his iPhone screen. The driver's lack of progress, coupled with this visual assault, formed a formidable headache in Steve's already frazzled mind.

"F-O-C-U-S!" he sternly whispered to himself as the humidity beneath his arms took on a life of its own, plotting to drench his shirt in an embarrassing fashion.

Just minutes away from the airport, Steve's phone pinged with a push notification from the airline, gleefully informing him of a terminal change. Cue internal expletives. With lightning speed, Steve frantically logged back into the Uber app, desperately attempting to switch the drop-off location. But alas, the travel gods had other plans, as a client suddenly posed a question directly to Steve during his Zoom call. Murphy's Law struck again.

Forced to focus on the call, Steve found himself squinting with the intensity of a radiologist in search of a hairline fracture, trying to decipher minuscule data sets on his phone screen magnified to a mind-boggling 1000%. In between his own comments, Steve resorted to a wild pantomime, flailing his arms and pointing frantically at his mobile device, desperately trying to convey the urgency of the terminal change to his oblivious driver. Yet, the driver remained steadfastly unresponsive, as if immune to Steve's wild gesticulations and pleas.

Defeated, Steve surrendered to the meeting, his voice masking the inner turmoil. "Of course, I'll get those edits back to you by the end of the day, 'consulting standard time,'" he declared, punctuating his statement with a finger-gun gesture pointed at his temple and silently mouthing "WTF" as they arrived at the wrong terminal. A text from his analyst appeared on his phone, a simple question: "PlzFix?" Steve laughed, typing back, "Yes. Hopefully, we're in the ninth inning with this client. At least you're on Pacific Time. I'll remember this come bonus time."

As the driver commenced unloading the vehicle, Steve reasoned that a language barrier must be at play, reluctantly deciding against leaving a two-star rating or withholding a tip. All he needed was a smooth journey through the "Super Priority" Pre-Check line at TSA, and he could still make his flight. Gathering his trusty Tumi roller bag and briefcase, Steve noticed some scuffs on the centrally placed, monogrammed patches that demanded near-term attention.

And then, it happened. Chernobyl erupted internally. The driver casually uttered, "Hold on a minute, I'm completing a drop-off." He nonchalantly removed his earbuds and bid Steve farewell with a deep voice and a noticeably Bostonian accent. "That mother$@#$#%$!! He ignored me for a personal call?! I'm at the WRONG terminal!" Suddenly, Steve channeled the essence of not one but two of Christian Bale's most iconic characters: Patrick Bateman's incredulous reaction to Paul Allen's business card and Batman's explosive encounter with The Joker in their final showdown.

With a fiery determination, Steve stormed towards the airport terminal; his gaze fixated forward and downward at a precise forty-five-degree angle. He huffed and puffed, treating the automatic doors as the final barrier to ending his personal nightmare. "Just one more obstacle," he grumbled inwardly. As the doors finally slid open, Steve's eyes darted around, scanning for any signs of progress.

And then he saw it—a cruel sight. The priority security line, firmly shut. A muffled curse slipped from his lips as he abruptly veered to the right, making a beeline for the gen-pop line, hoping it was shorter than the Nile. He fumbled to adjust both the driver's rating and tip downward on the Uber app, determined to vent his displeasure. Full steam ahead.

Suddenly, BAM! Steve found himself sprawled on the floor, a collision so sudden and unexpected that it left him utterly prostrate. So immersed in his phone, he had unwittingly collided with a woman whose stride could have clocked at twenty-five miles per hour, her momentum generating an impact that rivaled a heavyweight boxing match. Re-enter Susan.

The force of the collision sent Steve's suitcase and laptop bag crashing to the ground with such vigor that even the monogram patches jolted loose. "Guess I'll get those fixed before next week, after all," he thought as he tried to shake his head and the ringing from his ears. Meanwhile, an explosion of items continued to burst forth from Susan's bright blue Kate Spade purse, scattering like bouncing marbles across the gray terrazzo airport floors to distances that would make an Olympic shot putter green with envy. Each item seemed to possess a life of its own, bouncing and rolling with unbridled enthusiasm. Frustration seeped from the pores and eyes of both individuals as this encounter confirmed neither passenger would make that flight to Philadelphia. At last, their eyes met.

"And that, kids, is how I met your mother."

Yeah, right. If Susan and Steve were real people, we would have witnessed a viral showdown of epic proportions, with millions of viewers sharing the UFC-level verbal cage fight on every social media platform known to humanity. Even if they shared identical political views and cheered for the same sports teams, it no longer made an ounce of difference. At impact, they became sworn enemies, locked in an aviation setting for the next round of the Hunger Games. To each other, they were intruders, obstacles, Koopas – perhaps even Bowser.

Susan and Steve each diligently planned their trip. However, a series of unfortunate external events unfolded, culminating in the unexpected collision in a high-pressure moment. As a result, they both missed their flights, fingers pointed at one another. Preparation failed to produce the intended results. Similarly, we often pragmatically map out our careers. We put in the time, check off the right boxes, but external factors or internal politics seem to leave us just short of our desired endgame. When that occurs, it's all too easy to pin the blame and extend the index fingers in another's direction.

But what if Steve's eyes were not buried down toward the Uber app as he increased his pace in a heavily trafficked area? What if Susan paused the power ballad playing over her AirPods to hear the crescendoing stomp of hurried footsteps?

During air travel, there comes a point when we all question why a certain person seems to be in our way or, more interestingly, why they are behaving in such a manner. What if it was the behavior itself that we could define as "stranger?" Mark Twain famously stated, "Truth is stranger than fiction." He uses the word as an adjective rather than a noun. And in Twain's usage of the word, we see a very different meaning, one that is a bit less adversarial. Oxford defines the word in this capacity to mean "surprising, especially in a way that is difficult to understand." Can we avoid these "stranger" behaviors while we travel? And as we embark on our career journeys?

Yes, but to eliminate the surprise factor, it's best to know what to watch for along the way.

The Itinerary: Six Annoying Habits

In 1989, Stephen Covey unveiled *The Seven Habits of Highly Effective People*, sparking a revolution for legions desperate for a blueprint to personal and professional nirvana. Covey's mantra? Be proactive, own your actions, and live your values. He championed building meaningful relationships and mastering the art of the win-win. Admirable? Absolutely. Timeless? Without a doubt. Relatable? Well, let's just say if truth were a dartboard, Covey's book is a bullseye—for some.

Now, don't get me wrong—I'm not tossing Covey's magnum opus out with the kitchen sink. His insights are as noble as they are valuable. But here's my confession: I'm not always the epitome of Covey's effectiveness. There, I said it. Does that make me the villain in a self-help saga? Maybe. But I'll let you in on a little secret: My most profound life lessons haven't come from mastering effectiveness. No, they've come from the school of hard knocks. Therefore, it only makes sense to flip Covey's paradigm on its head.

Enter "The Six Habits of Highly Annoying Travelers." Through these habits, we encounter navigational beacons, approach paths, and runway lights and find that sometimes the best lessons are learned not by following in the footsteps of an effective leader but by observing a cautionary tale in the wild. Before we unveil the habits, please forgive the pre-recipe tirade.

First – I bet you're wondering, "Who is the guy writing this book, and why should I care about his perspective of random airport encounters?" Valid question. Unless you've read my chapter in *Leadership DNA* or Google searched "people with full names that read as funny sentences," you've likely never heard of me. I'm none of Usain Bolt, Simone Biles, Michael Phelps, Condoleezza Rice, or Jeff Bezos. I'm far more important than them, well, in two very select venues: 1) commercial airports and 2) Marriott hotels. At least in theory.

How? I ran the rat race and spun the hamster wheel, working in professional services for more than a decade as a consultant. Look down on me with mercy, all ye bankers and lawyers!

While his job duties were wildly inaccurate in *Up in the Air*, my weekly itineraries largely mirrored that of George Clooney in the film. But in my role, I fretted over clearing comments and up-or-out policies. I skied in panic mode to mountain-side lodges mid-vacation to join a client's Zoom meeting. I walked out the back of the church during Christmas Eve communion to field a managing director's persistent unanswered calls about a slide deck.

And what do I have to show for it? Besides my stellar vest collection, I'm now a million miler with one major US airline, and I also hold top-tier status with an additional domestic carrier. Who needs Super Bowl rings, Olympic hardware, Venus rosewater dishes, medals of freedom, or bricks of precious metals when there are luggage tags? Can't "Diamond" be anyone's best friend, or at least "Platinum?"

Speaking of Diamond, Delta Air Lines introduced its "Keep Climbing" slogan in 2010. It's a catchy tagline but a terrifying flight path, at least if applied literally. Sadly, we often apply the phrase in a literal sense to our career journeys. If I had to guess, I'd suggest that most readers of this book trend toward high levels of achievement and performance at work. By and large, we're very fortunate. That doesn't mean you don't feel as though you're in a holding pattern, running on a hamster wheel, or plateaued at some cruising altitude. Many of the firms and financial institutions we work at exacerbate this feeling thanks to an acute triangular org structure. You keep looking up, but it's difficult to keep climbing. Is there any more room at the top? Even if that's not your workplace environment, you're not immune. You've felt stuck and questioned why you felt lodged in your current position. It's all a bit of a rat race.

So, I'll re-ask my own question: why listen to me? One reason: I escaped the holding pattern. I leveraged that experience to find fulfilling work. That's not a slam on a long-term career in professional services; it just wasn't for me. But that didn't mean I didn't initially view myself as a failure. How did I finally shake that notion? I stopped looking straight up and shifted my sights outward. The new perspectives re-charted my flight path. Do I regret the circling? Not at all. It kept me airborne. And where I landed is where I needed to be. I love my job and rarely dread Mondays. That's a liberating feeling.

Let me clarify a few things. I don't smoke weed or micro-dose mushrooms. This book isn't about advocating for a life of minimalism or the virtues of renouncing all material possessions. I like nice things. Fortunately, I head the M&A engine for a private equity-backed company, so enjoying them is possible. But at the end of the day, I have fun at work, and I think others should, too. My goal is for these pages to provide my reflections as a way to stay sane as you get there, even if the path is a bit choppy en route.

Second – you're likely wondering who the perpetrators of these annoying habits are. Am I going to single out the slow pokes? Or the overzealous fast walkers? Yes, and yes. These habits have no bounds—they are committed by both the "road warriors" and the "plane averters."

At one end of the spectrum, we have the "road warrior," a frequent traveler who thrives on efficiency and privilege. Often found in the realms of professional services, these individuals strut through airports as if they hold full title to every terminal and commercial airplane in existence. They love boasting about their lightning-fast door-to-gate times and possess an uncanny ability to identify aircraft types for potential upgrade opportunities. Their favorite form of cardio is a late-year mileage "run" to maintain status. They can deduce your airline just by a casual mention of your departure, connection, or arrival cities, thanks to their encyclopedic knowledge of major airline hubs. These travelers are fiercely attached to their monogrammed belongings adorned with clanking metal tags that show their rank in the airline pecking order. They prefer to face a packed SoHo restaurant without a reservation rather than check a bag, regardless of the trip's duration. And let's not forget their astonishing expertise of airline lounges in each terminal at every airport, where they can recall every culinary offering, beverage selection, crowd level, Wi-Fi speed, seating arrangement, and even the availability of shower facilities before overnight flights. These self-proclaimed royals of the sky confidently navigate from security to the gate, always engrossed in calls, leaving no doubt of their elevated status. In the earlier story, think Steve.

At the other end of the spectrum, we have the "plane averter," a leisure/occasional traveler found in all walks of life. They embark on occasional work trips but mostly jet off for well-deserved vacations. Believing airports to be intricately designed to baffle and confuse, they find themselves perpetually puzzled by the multitude of security lines, boarding groups, and their ever-changing rules. "Why did I even bother to get that credit card if I'm boarding with everyone else?" Their bewilderment reaches new heights upon encountering the Analogic automated bin systems at major airport security stations, which seem to create more chaos than efficiency, as each passenger's bags become separated from one another as they enter the carousel. Naturally, they question the name itself, suspecting that "Analogic" must refer to the location of the brainpower of the genius who conceived such a system. Their minds are further perplexed by airlines' pricing strategies, charging for checked bags pre-departure, yet waiving the fee if bags are carried to the gate. They can't fathom why a middle seat just one row ahead in economy class commands an extra $40 each way. As they finally reach their gate and destination, these travelers feel a sense of relief and a touch of pity for those who endure such journeys on a regular basis. Think Susan.

Most readers likely fall into the first breed of travelers. You may have picked up this book with the hopes of discovering simple ways to avoid encounters with the latter category. I'm pleased to inform you that you can: request adoption into Logan Roy's fictitious family in *Succession* or join COP29 climate leaders and fly private.

Still, some other readers belong to the latter breed and may have purchased this book hoping for reviews of noise-canceling headphones, eye masks, or gadgets to fend off chatty seatmates. Alas, this is not a literary SkyMall (may it rest in peace). But if you simply desire to avoid those bothersome conversations, try maintaining a consistent stream of in-flight flatulence. Airport Mexican food should do just the trick. Or better yet, find a way to deduce your neighbor's political leanings and set your TV to the news station opposite their viewpoint.

Before we finally reach the habits, let's first explore some "stranger" actions that can be irksome but are not necessarily "surprising, in a way that is hard to understand." These occasional occurrences are often outside our control.

For example, nobody enjoys the cacophony of a wailing infant or the tyranny of a three-nager. However, we really should remember that the swaddled baby did not request to have their delicate ears subjected to 30,000 feet of pressure at a tender nine months of age. Likewise, the toddler and their weary parents did not ask for the FAA to seemingly conspire against them with an elongated taxi time, resulting in a tight connection that left no time for a Chick-fil-A pit stop and produced a hangry little tyke. We've all experienced the unwelcome prod from someone asking to cut in line at security because they received a last-call boarding notice. We've also likely found ourselves in situations where a meeting ran late, traffic thwarted our progress, and we desperately wanted to catch that final evening flight home. Or perhaps we were simply attempting to return a rental car at Chicago O'Hare.

Whether it's these behaviors or other situations like sprinting through concourses to make the final boarding call, jamming ourselves onto a terminal train as the doors shut and reopen, or blocking the walkway to quickly glance at the ineptly placed monitors, we must acknowledge that life happens. While annoying when encountered, the behaviors are understandable and relatable when you consider people desperately wanting to make it to their next destination. However, other behaviors fall well outside these boundaries.

Finally, we dive into the ingredients. If only I'd included a "Skip to Recipe" button from the outset. I give you The Six Habits of Highly Annoying Travelers:

1. The Gate Lice
2. The Backpack Wrecking Crew
3. The Overhead Tetris Flunkee
4. The Conference Call Deci-Bully
5. The Window Wobbler
6. The Eager Exiter

If these leave you scratching your head, fret not. If you feel a tinge of guilt, don't sweat. With each habit, we'll uncover a cautionary tale. And with each tale, we'll learn how to navigate the turbulence. We won't prevent delays or the occasional detours altogether, but with each habit, we will learn lessons that build upon each other and ultimately help each of us start the final approach to an intended destination, even if it's not a final one.

But let's slow down for just a second. Yes, I know, I also hate it when people walk without a purpose in the concourse. But baby steps, my friends. Before we can arrive at a destination, we first need a boarding pass to ensure our seat on the aircraft. And at the jet bridge, we learn that securing that seat isn't always so simple. It can get quite crowded in the boarding area. And so, on our first stop, we encounter the Gate Lice.

Habit 1: The Gate Lice

Gate Lice (*noun*): Specimens that possess an insatiable urge to congregate and swarm the boarding area before it is the designated time to board the aircraft. These creatures engage in a range of activities, including:

- Premature Congregating: Possesses an exceptional talent for gathering excessively early, as if the gate itself showcased the *Mona Lisa*. They disallow fellow passengers from boarding at the appropriate time.
- Boarding Zone Amnesia: Maintains astonishing inability to comprehend boarding announcements. They remain blissfully oblivious to their assigned boarding zone despite explicit and repeated instructions.
- The Bouncing Frenzy: Often engages in a curious bouncing ritual, eagerly inching closer to the boarding door with every lateral movement of the gate agent between computer screens and each minute closer to departure time.
- Boarding Line Oblivion: Abandons all semblance of decency when their designated boarding group is finally called and charge towards the boarding area like wildebeests after Mufasa.

The Fix: You Want to... But Probably Shouldn´t

Scan the area for open-toed shoes. Maneuver your luggage in a way that appears unintentional but is actually strategically aimed at the exposed toes when it is your time to board, like a comb going through hair after a Nix shampooing. Apologize with a gasp that rivals the "genuine" surprise of a celebrity accepting an award, all the while secretly savoring the delight in their squeals.

As Seen in the Terminal

The next time you fly from a major airline hub to New York City's LaGuardia airport on a Monday morning, take a look at the monitors in the gate area. You'll likely see an upgrade or priority list, that is, which is a list of passengers that fly so often that the airline will award them a first-class or premium economy seat if space is available. On a Monday morning flight with 200 seats, you'll likely notice up to eighty, ninety, or maybe even a hundred names. When gate agents call the priority boarding group, half of the gate area lines up in an orderly fashion to board the aircraft. These passengers move onto the plane like a brackish river of navy, charcoal, and gray attire flowing into the ocean. Often, passengers complete the entire boarding process in less than twenty minutes. While efficient, such a concentration of priority passengers means that even frequent flyers might end up with a middle seat. However, if you don't have mid-morning meetings in Manhattan, flights in the early afternoon provide an alternative to the seat crunch as they usually attract fewer business travelers and thus offer more preferable seats. Swap out the sea of navy, charcoal, and gray attire for "I Heart NYC" t-shirts. You'll still see names dotting the monitors, but far more will appear on the "stand-by" list waiting for seat clearance and a boarding pass rather than a seat upfront.

On a mundane Monday in the fall of 2019, I took the 1:00 p.m. flight from Hartsfield-Jackson International Airport in Atlanta, GA, to LaGuardia. My schedule worked out well—I had Monday morning meetings in Atlanta and Tuesday morning meetings at 21st & Park. To my delight, the airline upgraded me to first class the night before due to seat availability. I would have ample arm space to use my laptop and position it in such a way that my neighbor could not view my screen. Yes, I had a privacy screen, but I still didn't trust it. But let's leave those trust issues to my therapy sessions rather than these pages. That aside, I was very excited about this trip and the materials I needed to review. The reading? A CIM for an acquisition target I had sourced and gotten into our deal pipeline myself. CIM stands for Confidential Information Memorandum. You know those brochures that realtors put together for your house when it's listed to showcase the highlights? Investment bankers put together similar documents for the businesses they take to market for sale, albeit far lengthier and with financial data massaged like a St. Regis spa patron. This particular business, once we acquired it, would truly transform our company's product offering and help shield some of our exposure to some recently levied tariffs on certain foreign goods in our portfolio. I found this target; it was my baby—I was stoked.

Another benefit of flying at non-peak times? Smaller crowds at security and generally throughout the airport. Hell, you might even find a seat after taking just one lap around the airline lounge or an airport bar. These benefits materialized on this particular Monday, and I swiftly passed through security well ahead of schedule. After five minutes of irrationally scrutinizing the lounge's banana selection for a fruit without bruises, I finally found one and grabbed it. Off to the gate. The basis for the trip, plus the smooth airport process, had me on Cloud 9 even before the plane ascended and without a single milligram of Adderall to boot.

As I approached the gatehouse, a sudden urge to douse myself head to toe in permethrin washed over me. There they were, the hoard of gate lice gathered so close to the boarding door that it became almost impossible to see the door or the gate agent station. If you were in a different setting, you might think a crowd of paparazzi had just spotted a Kardashian or the latest offspring of Nick Cannon. The horror on my face didn't go unnoticed by a fellow passenger, who had similar luggage tags affixed to her bags, which meant she sympathized with my nonsensical disgust. With a laugh, she informed me that the 12:00 p.m. flight to LaGuardia had been canceled due to a mechanical issue. That meant these parasites would be crawling all over the gate area to clamor for a seat on our flight. Standby lice! My skin started to itch.

Equally frustrated but with actual reason, the gate agent grabbed her device and made an announcement, her voice filled with exasperation. "Ladies and gentlemen, I am once again asking you to please, pretty please, back up. The arriving plane has just landed, and we need to deplane the passengers and clean the aircraft before we can begin boarding. The passengers who were delayed need a clear pathway to the terminal to avoid missing their connections. If you were on the earlier canceled flight, please refer to the video monitors. All seat assignments will be confirmed and displayed on the screen. Thank you for flying with us, and we appreciate your patience and loyalty."

The crowd let out an audible groan as if the kicker for their favorite NFL team had just missed a game-tying field goal wide right at the end of regulation. They attempted to follow the agent's instructions, but they stood so tightly packed together that their movement was severely restricted. They bounced and shuffled slightly apart. The pathway they created for exiting passengers seemed to assume that the inbound flight was filled with tiny children or adults with severe eating disorders. "Better restock those barf bags." Finally, the door swung open, and delayed passengers rushed into the terminal, causing the gate lice to disperse quickly and widely. Most of them, but not all.

Amidst the sea of gate lice, there was one young man in his early twenties who seemed particularly stubborn and unwilling to move away from the gate. His name was Brian. Positioned just three feet from the door, he stood directly behind the pole divider that separated the priority and main boarding lanes into two sections. Brian remained undeterred by the people deplaning, who repeatedly bumped into his backpack adorned with the logo of a Big 4 firm. For context, the term "Big 4" refers to the four largest accounting firms that offer audit, tax, and advisory (i.e., consulting) services. Based on Brian's choice of a firm logo-emblazoned bag instead of a personally monogrammed one, it was safe to assume he was a new hire.

Seeking refuge, I managed to find a small crevice to the right of the boarding area, nestled between the windows and the handicapped seating. It allowed me to stand completely out of the way and strategically avoid the gradually recongregating masses of gate lice. As the incoming flight finished deplaning, the gate agent gestured for Brian to come over. I wondered if he would comply, given his persistent squatting tactics of the past fifteen minutes, but to my surprise, he obliged. I didn't intend to eavesdrop, but the volume of the gate agent's voice left me with no alternative.

"Hi there. What's your name, dear?" the gate agent asked, waving Brian over.

"Brian Sanderson," he replied, slowly lowering the straps of his backpack off his shoulders and grasping them with his hands. It seemed he was bracing for bad news.

"Thank you," she typed away on her device. "Okay, Mr. Sanderson, I hate to break it to you, but this flight is now oversold, and we have fifty-four people on the standby list. Unfortunately, you're at the bottom, so it's highly unlikely that you'll make it onto this flight. Would you mind taking a seat away from the boarding area, and I'll check for later flights to LaGuardia once we finish getting these folks onboard?"

Before Brian could ask the question she had undoubtedly heard countless times, she interjected, "You're automatically listed on the next flight out if you don't make this one."

Brian's demeanor and tone sank dramatically. "Thank you. I'm just a bit confused. My friend works for the airline and gave me a buddy pass. Just a few hours ago, he told me that this flight had thirty-five open seats and only twelve people were on the standby list. I even confirmed it with the ticketing agent when I arrived at the airport this morning. Did I do something wrong to be moved to the bottom of the list?"

The gate agent's empathy grew as she realized that one of her fellow employees had subjected poor Brian to this situation without proper warning. "No, no, not at all, sir. We had to cancel the flight to LaGuardia right before this one due to mechanical issues, and some of those passengers were given priority placement on this flight since they were paying customers. That's why you've seen a change in your position and the number of available seats. There were 187 of them, and most of them won't make this flight either, so we're trying to accommodate those passengers first and ensure they can still get home today on the remaining flights from here into New York."

"So, that means I probably won't make it to New York City today?"

"I can't say for certain without looking at the flight loads, but I wouldn't make any dinner reservations. I promise I'll help you look once we get this flight out."

Before Brian could even return to the seating area, the pilot attempted to inconspicuously open the boarding door to inform the gate agent that catering was running behind schedule but on its way. The pilot estimated that the crew would need an additional ten to fifteen minutes before they would be ready to commence boarding. Brian paused. The gate agent made a face and accompanying grunt that indicated she was well aware of the incoming response from the passengers in the boarding area despite the minor delay. Nevertheless, she had no choice but to convey the information to them. She did so over the PA system, eliciting two typical responses: 1) a more exaggerated, collective groan than before, now akin to the sound a golden retriever makes when it can't reach its ball under the sofa, and 2) a line forming in front of the gate agent as passengers inquired whether she possessed the extraordinary ability to gauge their bladder capacity and determine if fifteen minutes would afford them sufficient time to use the restrooms before boarding. It was at that moment when Brian became a welcome distraction.

She called Brian back to the desk and began exploring alternative flight options. Her facial expressions, accompanied by fervent typing on her keyboard, conveyed the dreaded answer to Brian before she even uttered a word. "So... LaGuardia is completely booked for today, but let me check JFK... nope, not good. Alright, how about Newark? Hmm, not looking promising either. Oh, let's see if there's anything available at White Plains... Ah, there's a seat... but it's on a regional jet... and there are already 16 people on the standby list."

Brian's head dropped in defeat, but the pilot, who was lingering near the boarding door, chimed in, "Why don't you try Philadelphia and take the train up to New York City? The train departs right from the airport and takes you to Penn Station. It's only about an hour and a half ride."

"You could also fly to Reagan in DC and train for about three hours," a nearby passenger blurted aloud. I guess I wasn't the only person eavesdropping.

"Well, how about that! Those are some pivots! Let... me ... look, ok! There are sixteen open seats on the 2:15 flight to Philadelphia and only ten people on the standby list. If that works for you, I can make the switch. Just be ready to boogie—that flight departs from Terminal B, so you'll need to hustle." The printer sounded as Brian gazed at the incoming paper boarding pass. The door beeped as the pilot walked back down the jet bridge.

Brian quickly sent a text to his friends in New York City, informing them of the new plan. The pivot. He might miss out on some evening activities, but at least he had not packed his suitcase in vain. He would be in New York before the day was over. With the authority of Moses, Brian made his final move at Gate A31, turning around and confidently parting the crowd of people as if he were splitting the Red Sea. Once through, the gate lice immediately receded to their prior positions, blocking the first group called aboard and extending the boarding delay.

As Applied in Reality

Time to Take a Trip

What can we learn from Brian's story? Other than to never accept non-revenue travel vouchers and buddy passes. In Milton Friedman's own words, "There's no such thing as a free lunch." Or free flight.

Brian's story teaches us the importance of setting a goal (a destination like Manhattan), preparing for the journey (packing and timely making it to the airport), and remaining flexible and open to advice (listening to gate agents and pilots) so that we can pivot to end up where we ultimately need to be (the flight to Philadelphia). And as we try to do this? Well, expect people pushing, shoving and crowding every step of the way.

Undoubtedly, you've experienced the swarm of gate lice in your own travels. Passengers pile into compact areas and block access to a plane. All too often, they're in a later boarding group or still waiting on a seat. Lengthy boarding and crowded concourses result in flight delays, missed connections, or arriving at your gate just to find the boarding door closed. Such events keep us in those never-ending mid-air banks and turns.

Our professional journeys parallel this scenario. People block our paths to board, even when it's our turn. Other times, people outrank us and land seats on flights headed towards career destinations we thought were ours. Fortunately, gate agents and pilots exist in our professional endeavors – we must look for them to find ways to secure seats on alternative routes. By doing so, we learn that crucial skill, the pivot.

I had to learn this, too. And it wasn't easy or quick. I embarked on my adventure, focused squarely on flights headed towards a career destination akin to Manhattan, fixated on only one airport and one flight. Okay, maybe two.

Selecting a Destination: Manhattan

Brian wanted to arrive in Manhattan that evening in time for dinner with friends. Brian thankfully resolved his flight issue and learned to pivot to reach his destination in a matter of hours. He made it to New York City that evening, even if it was a late meal. Me? Well, try several decades.

It started when I was a kid. Let me preface: I was not a normal child. You see, my initial Manhattan was dreams of Olympic medals as a gymnast, fixating on the 2000 Sydney Games and keeping 2004 as my "plan B." Imagine the inner turmoil when my grand ambitions faced a major roadblock: I excelled only in floor exercise and vault, and even on those events, I just really wasn't that good. I was the "Group 9" gymnast crowding the gate as the premier status passengers tried to board. With only seven athletes making the Olympic team every four years at the time, and hundreds outperforming me each year and that number growing, even a sociology major could calculate my slim chances of standing on an Olympic podium.

By age thirteen, I'd come to terms with the reality that I wouldn't board my Olympic flight. It was a depressing realization. I say this only to highlight I was born so Type-A that I demanded pressed clothes rather than the swaddling variety upon my delivery. Thankfully, my despondency over these harrowing hardships lasted only a year, cured by something as profound as the film *Jerry Maguire*.

Yes, that's right. My new Manhattan? The completely realistic and accessible career field of sports agency and management. I suppose, by comparison, it was more realistic – but still within the margin of error in a swing state.

Fortunately, by the time I reached my senior year of high school, I'd outgrown the *Jerry Maguire* dream and evaluated universities like a normal teenager, except that I hadn't. No, I looked at college options exclusively based in major media hub cities teeming with professional sports teams. I narrowed my choices to Pepperdine University outside Los Angeles and Southern Methodist University (SMU) in Dallas.

I boasted a credible high school resume, top-notch grades, and SAT scores within the target thresholds of all the schools where I applied. Unfortunately, *Full House's* Aunt Becky wasn't available to fund my application process, and I received an envelope from Pepperdine skinnier than a 1990s Calvin Klein model. Gate lice? Here? Where did I rank in these boarding groups?

While I didn't realize it at the time, the rejection was probably one of the biggest blessings in disguise as it led me to SMU. Here, and through this institution, my dreams of Manhattan finally became a reality, but more on that much later.

A fun side note, *Jerry Maguire* begins with Tom Cruise desperately seeking to sign the hottest quarterback sensation, Frank "Cush" Cushman. Portrayed by Jerry O'Connell, Cush actually hailed from SMU, a discovery that I stumbled upon roughly three months after enrollment as if the universe conspired to affirm my path. There was no going back.

Ticket Type: Buddy Pass or Boarding Pass?

If you're not familiar, SMU sits in the heart of Dallas, just two blocks off a major interstate exit. You can see the city's skyline clearly from the top floor of the campus' iconic Dallas Hall. Despite its proximity to downtown, nothing about the school grounds screams urban. SMU consistently earns high rankings on "Most Beautiful Campus" lists across numerous publications, and for good reason. Once one turns onto Bishop Boulevard, the campus' main artery, a person no longer feels as though they are in a metropolitan area. Large trees overhang and shade the roadways and grassy median between the looping roadway. The timeless red brick paired with Corinthian columns creates a perfectly consistent Georgian Colonial aesthetic across dormitories, academic buildings, sports venues, museums, chapels, and yes - even the parking garages. It's a place to dream big. And that, I did.

Many of my classmates took advantage of the connections fostered by SMU in the consulting, investment banking, commercial real estate, and other financial sectors that yielded high-income-earning jobs after graduation. They secured boarding passes. They accepted offers and selected seats through traditional recruiting methods. They knew their destinations and flight numbers. I flirted with opportunities, but in my head and my gut, those planes just wouldn't get me to Manhattan. I was tunnel-visioned on LaGuardia: sports agency. Who needed PHL or DCA, or the MBB (McKinsey, Bain, BCG), the Big 4, or Wall Street, when you thought you could sign the next José Altuve or golf's version of "Cush," SMU's Bryson DeChambeau right out of the gates? And to be fair, my vest collection was already matured, given my stature as an SMU frat boy. But the major issue? No formal recruiting process for a career in sports agency. I was Brian, relying on a buddy pass, and for a spot to open so I could make my flight. How crowded could my flight be?

Preparing for the Career Journey

Brian packed his bags, arrived on time and made his way to the gate ready to board the plane. He positioned himself ahead of the other gate lice. I needed to do the same if I wanted to become Jerry Maguire. But how? In the film, Tom Cruise's character informs us he paved the way to a career in sports management through law school. So, pre-law it was. I decided to major in English given its reputation for producing the highest LSAT scorers. My pragmatic parents demanded I also major in a subject matter that would lead to actual employment.

I realized what truly fascinated me about the job went beyond the prospect of rubbing shoulders with top-tier athletes. I wanted to delve into their personalities, understand their unique brands, and align them with suitable products or services for sponsorship. It was the art of effective, quasi-corporate matchmaking, a skill set that screamed one thing: marketing and advertising. With a nod of approval from my parents, I embarked on the double major path.

While in college, I also tailored my activities and résumé to the job. I held the reins of social chairman for three years. In my mind, I needed to understand how to curate guest lists and throw serious bangers if I wanted to attract and maintain clients. We all saw how Ari Gold operated in *Entourage*; I needed to follow in his footsteps. Maybe minus the paintball scene. Poor Lloyd.

Okay, I held other leadership positions, too. I even received some university awards, and as a result, some hardware. Take that, Sydney Olympics. Outside the campus, I landed summer internships at Baker Botts in Houston. The firm's namesake boasted political prowess in several presidential administrations, but I was more interested in the fact that one of the senior partners at the firm negotiated NBA legend Yao Ming's contracts. I wanted to see how the law and sports met at the crossroads professionally. And put that on my CV.

I was Brian, at the front of the gate house, just waiting to hear my name called. I had the right credentials on my résumé, the relevant reference letters, the required GPA, and my LSAT practice test scores aligned with my targeted school's ranges. There was no way the gate lice would crowd me out at this turn. I pre-submitted my applications so each institution would receive my test score. I pre-paid the fees, took the test, and waited.

No Seat for You on This Flight

And then I got the email—it was no Elle Woods moment from *Legally Blonde*. I scored a 150 on the LSAT, a whopping 15 points below my practice average. The difference felt as vast as dog years to human years. Somehow, I landed uncompetitively in the 44th percentile. Some law schools even offered reimbursements for my applications. No, of course they didn't.

"Yikes, that's—well... I'm so sorry," said the law firm partner I interned for that summer, his sympathy echoing the tone reserved for someone who just lost a beloved dog. Well, unless you're South Dakota's Kristi Noem.

LSAT takers and applicants moved up and down the admissions lists. Those who missed their marks, but still tested competitively, mirrored the passengers who were originally on the cancelled flight and feverishly wanted on Brian's segment. The gate lice took spots at the schools where I'd hoped to attend.

Despite the odds, Brian still believed he could make it to NYC as he stood at the gate before they broke the bad news. I was in a similar head space. Meredith, my college best friend, and I clung to the hope that SMU would recognize my dedication and overlook the LSAT score. On her birthday, the rejection from Dedman School of Law arrived, surprising no one but us. At dinner that night, as her parents inquired about my law school plans, the waiter's timely service of a gin and tonic—tonic on the side—saved me from a rare case of tears. I nearly choked on the piney potion before realizing it was a mix-it-yourself affair. The next morning, nursing a hangover, I pondered, "What the hell am I to do?"

You're probably thinking, "Thank God. He talked to some folks, his gate agent and pilot, wised up, and decided not to go to law school to pursue some ridiculous dream.

You'd think so, but you'd be wrong—very wrong. No, I doubled down. Imagine if Brian had returned to his home that day but tested his luck on a different weekend. That's what I did, just a year later. In the interim, I worked at Baker Botts and read the autobiographical works of Leigh Steinberg and Drew Rosenhaus. Evidently, both real-life agents inspired many parts of *Jerry Maguire*. Drew Rosenhaus' *A Shark Never Sleeps* showcased his rise using strong ties to Miami football and his alma mater, and that's when it clicked.

I'd gone about the process all wrong. I needed to attend law school that produced athletes that could line my future client roster. SMU hadn't yet started its football renaissance, so I set my sights on the Southeastern Conference for better prospects.

Thicker packets finally arrived this admissions cycle. I'd parted with some of the gate lice. Attracted by the legendary coach Steve Spurrier's recent arrival at the University of South Carolina, I saw an opportunity to join a program in its budding phase—much like Rosenhaus himself. In the late summer of 2006, I packed my bags for Columbia, South Carolina, choosing my law school based on the hiring of a football coach—100% to further pursue a career I chose based on a film. What could go wrong?

Wait, I'm Still at the Airport?

Learning that my admissions to law school meant I was still Brian at the airport waiting for a flight to a career in sports agency was quite sobering. In law school, yet again, no formal recruiting process existed to break into this field, so I was still holding just a buddy pass. Group 9? Hell, I hadn't even been assigned a zone yet.

Imagine those stagnant ponds you eye and instinctively associate with malaria breeding grounds—that's law school, just substitute malaria with mental illness. As the reality of my career prospects settled in, I caught the bug. The odd thing about law school administrations is they expect students to want to practice law and do so in the state where they attend. Insanity. It baffled me that there was no directory that highlighted athlete hot spots or opportunities for social introductions.

Okay, I wasn't that naive, but the NCAA's updated bylaws thwarted a Rosenhaus-like rise. And the intensity of law school left little time for external social interactions. For me, the ROI on law school's price tag dwindled by the day, but my luck seemed to change before my second year concluded. An in-person interview awaited me with a boutique sports agency in Orange County, California. This was it. I was next in line. My buddy ticket was converting into a boarding pass.

The firm's client list intensified my excitement. It was so spectacular I did a double take, thinking I'd stumbled upon the ESPY Awards' attendee list. High-caliber coaches dotted the roster like sprinkles on a cake otherwise composed of NFL players.

After the interview, I thought I'd finished a round of golf seven under at Augusta National on Masters Sunday. We seemed to connect on multiple levels, and they seemed genuinely impressed with my unconventional approach to my law school selection process. As I left the building, buoyed by their final words— "We'll be in touch soon"—I allowed myself to believe, perhaps for the first time in a long while, I'd hear my name called, cleared to board the aircraft.

But they would not be in touch soon. As days stretched into weeks with no response to my thank you notes, my high hopes quickly dimmed. I sent one last follow-up, like a desperate note to someone on Tinder who never meant to swipe right on your profile in the first place. Nothing. No response.

I mused bitterly as I despondently recounted a decade-long pursuit. Somehow, here, at the boarding door, another gate louse outranked me in my quest for the seat. Like Brian, I found myself desperately needing friendly faces to help me pivot and find a flight to Philly. Or just someone to slap the crap out of and sense into me.

Fortunately, I found the former.

Finding the Gate Agent and Pilot

Professor Lad called students to the front of the room each class, much like the gate agent did to Brian. My first trip to the chalkboard occurred in the fall of 2007.

Professor Lad noticed my consistent enrollment in every class he taught each semester. Sixteen total credit hours under his tutelage—a small crew of us joked that we minored in "Lad." Embodied in Professor Lad was the understated dignity, wit, and sharpness of a true Southern gentleman. A South Carolina native, he seemed equally comfortable in either a bow tie or a casual golf polo.

His head often glistened under the fluorescent classroom lighting. At about 5'8", he maintained a slender frame thanks to his passion for cycling.

While he did not tower behind the podium, he commanded a great deal of respect in the classroom. He routinely assigned "problems" so that students could apply legal doctrine to "solve" a practical issue and understand the material. Professor Lad never mocked or ridiculed a student for incorrect answers; he taught extremely difficult subject matter, but he expected preparation. His ability to detect the difference between genuine confusion and blatant disregarding of assignments made some of us question if he maintained a dual-career path with the CIA. If he detected the latter, you left the classroom. No ifs, ands, or buts.

The first encounter with Professor Lad's policy involved a fellow classmate, Daniel Jones, just two weeks into class. Daniel whined and protested that he should stay in class simply because he paid for it. Oof.

"Mr. Jones," Professor Lad said calmly while pulling his round eyeglasses partially down his nose. "So did your classmates, and they came here to learn. Your lack of preparedness thwarts that. Respect them and leave. Now."

Daniel raised his voice, but it met Professor Lad's elevated hand and voice. "You are dismissed. You can return to class on Thursday when you've prepared."

Mr. Jones slammed his book and huffed out of the room. Naturally, Professor Lad looked down at his roster, then towards me. It was my turn to work through the problem.

"Well, Mr. Blewett, you're up. Fortunately for you, the bar was set gratuitously low," he said with a friendly smirk and pushed his glasses back to their proper position. "C'mon down."

Thankfully, I'd read that day. Like I said, Professor Lad never intended to shame. He simply set expectations and held students accountable to those standards. He made you want to perform, and I really needed that at that time.

Professor Lad primarily taught tax law courses. Law schools typically require only one semester of basic income tax law, as most law students are allergic to math. When I compared schedules with friends, their incredulous looks suggested they believed I willingly subjected myself to private waterboarding sessions at Guantanamo Bay conducted personally by Vice President Dick Cheney. To date, that still sounds way better than torts. 'Merica.

Frequent office hours visits involved career advice more so than explanations of difficult code sections.

"Maybe you should consider some career options in tax given the number of courses you've taken. Lotsa folks chasin' sports dreams that can't pay their bills." A different flight destination? Newark? White Plains? He gave me options, as though listing off airports as the agent did for Brian.

If Professor Lad was the gate agent, then Professor Brant was certainly the pilot. Professor Brant, a rising star among the faculty, earned a reputation for being one of the sharpest young minds the school had recently employed. Yet he somehow remained remarkably approachable and sociable. He always made a point to greet us when he ran into our gym-rat crew during our workouts.

Like Professor Lad, Professor Brant primarily focused on tax law, but he took a slightly gentler approach in the classroom. His classes initially drew larger crowds than usual for tax, thanks to thinly veiled crushes held by our female classmates. The numbers often dwindled right before the drop-add deadline as students uncovered the topics included in the readings. Imagine that, a tax class... about tax.

Corporate Tax was no different, and a small group-like discussion on corporate spin-offs sparked a discussion about the tax advisory practices at Big 4 firms. To my surprise, I learned that these firms post-Enron didn't exclusively hire CPAs; they also valued law degrees. I hate to admit this, but I spent the remainder of class surfing the web to look at the various tax advisory practices at these firms.

Crucially, the firms boasted practices that supported, yes, sports teams and leagues. Subsequent discussions with both professors supported this shift in my job search. They even believed this would be a strong match, given my law school curriculum. Recruiters affirmed the strategy and began to set up interviews. I was moving up the lists, beating out the gate lice. And there it was, my flight to Philadelphia. Suddenly, that final year, I realized that missing the flight to one airport didn't mean missing my destination altogether. A different route could still bring me to where I wanted to be. It just might take a little longer.

In other words, I'd finally learned to pivot, parted the gate lice, and found myself a seat on a plane.

Boarding for Philadelphia

I'm not sure who'll take more offense to the comparison—tax professionals or Philadelphians—but hey, I've been the former and spent weeks on end in the latter, so I've earned the right to make it. I also get that some of you are probably shaking your heads, thinking that a Big 4 tax job is hardly a consolation prize when the goal was *Jerry Maguire*. I'm not running for higher office, so I'm not going to sell you that bullshit. But stick with me—this is just the first habit, and it took Brian a flight, a train ride, a cab from Penn Station, and a walk in the rain without an umbrella before he finally ended up at dinner with friends.

In retrospect, basing an entire career plan on a work of fiction probably isn't best practice. But here's the thing—what looks like a dead-end might just be a pivot waiting to happen. You just need to look around for the gate agents and pilots who can help you find another way. To me, that lesson was vital. I learned to seek them out at every step of the journey. And believe me, I had to part my fair share of gate lice—those people who crowd you out at every shift and turn. But I made it to my destination, even if it didn't happen on my timeline or look quite like I imagined. And yes, that part required extensive therapy.

I get it—rejection sucks, whether it's at your dream school, program, job, firm, company, or industry. Maybe it's even all of the above, each one causing the next. But if you're willing to pivot, and willing to seek out advice from people who want to help, I think you'll be surprised. I'll admit, it's hard to keep that perspective when you're in the thick of it, but that's why there are more chapters in this book. Fortunately, the second habit—the backpack wrecking crew—has a lot more to say on that subject.

And yeah, I know—I spoiled my current career role in the first chapter. But did I get the dream sports gig, too? Well, let's just say I think it worked out, but you'll have to stick around to find out how.

Chapter 4

Habit 2: The Backpack Wrecking Crew

Backpack Wrecking Crew (*noun*): A distinct breed known for inflicting unsuspecting passengers with a mixture of irritation, discomfort, and sometimes pain. Usually engaged in activities that showcase their disregard for personal space and general principles of travel etiquette. The exploits include:

- Wrecking Balls: Casually dons a backpack perched precariously on a single shoulder while firmly gripping a second piece of luggage with both hands, ensuring any potential mishaps or swinging impacts to fellow passengers cannot be mitigated.
- Airbus Assaults: Navigates the narrow aisle undeterred by the confines of the aircraft cabin with an unparalleled confidence and ignorance of spatial awareness. Frequently spin unapologetically, ensuring that every innocent bystander gets a front-row seat to a fresh black eye.
- Kneecap Combat: Takes a seat with a peculiar twist, causing knees to invade the lower seat back of the passenger ahead with intense ferocity.

The Fix: You Want to... But Probably Shouldn't

Closely monitor entrants during the boarding process. Assume the prime defensive position, with your upper body ready for action. When the backpack swings your way, raise your shoulder or fists and redirect the force back at them, resulting in a stumble of epic proportions.

As Seen on the Aircraft

Most airlines have jumped on the "premium" economy bandwagon, typically placing these seats in the first four to five rows immediately following first class. While these seats may come with free booze, better snacks, and a few extra inches of legroom, for those in aisle seats, the perks kick in only after the boarding chaos subsides.

Let's first examine the front row of this premium economy cabin, a.k.a. the "firing line." You see, first-class cabins typically seat two passengers per side, and then it transitions to three passengers per side. This shift not only alters the aisle width but also messes with the row numbering. So, while the last row of first class might be row four, suddenly, you find yourself in row ten in premium economy. It's no wonder passengers start turning around to ask flight attendants or fellow passengers in an attempt to double-check their seat location. These movements cause little commotion in the wider aisles of the first-class cabin, but once passengers spill into economy and twirl, if you're seated in the aisle – bring your hard hat and safety goggles.

Similar to Monday morning flights, Thursday evening flights also attract a swarm of business travelers. Those in the consulting world often jet off to client sites on Monday mornings and return home every Thursday. Since most passengers expense these flights to their companies or clients, airlines take advantage of their price insensitivity by charging higher fares. If you've ever tried booking a long weekend getaway to a major airline hub, you probably noticed steep fares if you dared to depart between 4:00 p.m. and 7:30 p.m. on a Thursday afternoon. The Rosetta Stone of air travel pricing? Cracked.

Finally, the long week in mid-December reached its pinnacle — Thursday afternoon, the time to head home from Bloomington, IL. Miraculously, no snow was in the forecast, almost ensuring an on-time journey. Although the Bloomington airport was small, every major US airline served it, thanks to the city housing one of the largest insurance companies in the country. The fares to and from this city on Monday mornings and Thursday afternoons rivaled international flight fares. Since flights outside these peak times likely carried only a handful of passengers, the airlines needed to recoup their revenues when there were more passengers.

The aircraft types used for flights to and from Bloomington are commonly referred to as "regional" jets. Major airlines contract with smaller carriers to operate specific routes, sometimes due to demand and sometimes due to runway capacity. The contracted airlines typically paint their planes to resemble the larger carriers (also known as livery). Their crew dons similar attire and even announces the flight number in conjunction with the airline you booked with. The planes generally accommodate fifty to ninety passengers. If you've never flown on one, your assumption is correct — less capacity for passengers results in a less spacious interior.

The overhead bins on regional jets can only accommodate smaller rollerboards and often struggle to fit large backpacks or duffel bags, depending on how they are packed. However, the cabin configuration is the most crucial aspect to envision in your mind. As you enter the plane, the first-class cabin seats one passenger on the right side of the aisle and two passengers on the left side. In contrast, the economy cabin seats two passengers on each side of the aisle. This odd-to-even switch in the seat pattern creates a narrow, diagonal angle (highlighted by the lighted path) that exposes the first economy aisle seat on the left, almost as if the passenger is seated in the middle of the boarding lane.

As passengers wriggle through the diagonal turn of the tight cabin to find their seat, the person in that unfortunate seat feels like they're subjected to a dull guillotine, enduring constant bumps and nudges to their head and neck region without the courtesy of swift execution. Unfortunately for Samantha Weber, she drew the unlucky card of this "premium" seat on that winter afternoon's flight. I was fortunately in the window seat next to her, offering "premium" viewership to the show that unfolded. Who doesn't love a matinee?

When Ms. Weber boarded the plane, she deftly maneuvered through the narrow aisle and reached her seat next to me. She graciously ignored me, wasted no time, and immediately opened her laptop, determined to finish a work assignment before the boarding door closed. Samantha likely knew that sitting defenseless in this seat with her laptop ablaze was not the wisest choice.

"Nevertheless, she persisted."

As Samantha diligently focused on her email, the boarding process unfolded around her. The first encounter occurred with a disheveled man engrossed in a phone call. He used his left hand to hold his phone, wires tangled from the device up to his headphones. The man's right hand shouldered a garment bag, only partially zipped and clothes poking out. He smelled of "Desperate Rush," the latest scent creation from Tom Ford (joking, don't waste a Google search). And he wore it with the confidence of a sixteen year old bestowed with his first bottle of Aqua di Gio. Oblivious to his surroundings, he awkwardly made the diagonal turn between first class and coach, causing his laptop bag to slip off his right shoulder. Like a demolition ball headed towards an abandoned skyscraper, it struck Samantha's ThinkPad and slammed shut the machine. Unfazed, the man continued his call, completely unaware of the impact he had just caused. Samantha sat there shocked and aghast, refraining from turning around to glare at him like Cersei Lannister after exacting her revenge.

The next encounter involved a young passenger wearing a backpack. It was stuffed to the brim and protruded almost two feet behind her. She was clearly not going to fork over those baggage fees. It was unclear whether she was a breathing billboard or just newly employed, as her hat, shirt, and bags all donned a company logo. Sporting a lanyard around her neck, she seemed to be early in her career and headed to some type of onboarding conference.

"Wow, this plane is tiny! How do you fit anyone on here comfortably?" asked the young passenger.

"You'd be surprised. We make the most of the space we have. Sorry we couldn't transport you in your corner office. Maybe next time," the flight attendant politely and affably said aloud. "This is no smaller than your cubicle, sweetie," she thought internally as she tightened the grip of her hands clasped behind her back.

Samantha heard none of this interaction and fervently typed away. But she couldn't ignore the passenger for long. At the diagonal turn, the human billboard swung around 180 degrees, backpack still on her back, to address her colleague behind her and proclaim her doubts about their bags fitting in the overhead space. As she turned, her backpack collided into Samantha's face like a Wipeout obstacle and knocked her glasses to her lap as though they were a failed contestant. I thought an imprint of the corporate logo on the passenger's backpack would soon appear on Samantha's cheek. She should've seen it coming, but she didn't.

The impact also knocked Samantha's laptop to the floor, prompting her to unleash a stream of expletives and exclaim, "Seriously?! Why?! I just need to send this one email!" Oblivious to her own actions, the new-hire wrecking ball made a snide comment, saying, "Maybe finish it at the office. You don't own the plane," as she waltzed to her seat.

I waited for a reaction, but Ms. Weber simply composed herself and returned to her email response. With the boarding process nearly complete, passengers entered the plane spaced one or two entrants every few minutes. Samantha thought she was in the clear. "Ten uninterrupted minutes before they tell me to stow my laptop," she thought. Of course, she was wrong.

It was not the sight of him but the smell that announced his arrival. A man somehow smuggled what smelled like kimchi through security. The cabin was small enough that even if he sat at the rear of the aircraft, the nostrils in row one would weep.

His seat assignment? Directly behind Samantha and, by default, me. He struggled to navigate the boarding process, holding shopping bags and food items in his hands. He donned an excessively large duffle bag on his back. He didn't seem to know what he was doing despite attempting too many tasks at one time. Attempting to squeeze into the cramped seat without spilling his food, he sat down while still wearing his duffle. He hit the seat cushion with such force that his knees rammed into Ms. Weber through the back of her chair. She throttled forward as her seat belt nearly caused whiplash.

The impact not only knocked Samantha's laptop into the aisle but also sent her phone and glasses scurrying forward, disappearing underneath the seats in front of her. Samantha had it. With frustration boiling within her, Samantha couldn't help but unleash her pent-up irritation. She turned around to confront the man, only to meet his indignant look of aggression. He defensively shouted, "Turn around, ma'am. I paid for this seat!"

She snapped, "So did I, and it was probably much more expensive than yours, you prick!" An accurate statement, though a bit lacking in decorum. Samantha was ready for a Presidential primary debate. A brief and awkward silence enveloped the aircraft as Samantha searched for her items, and the boarding door closed, accompanied by a resonant "thud."

As they so often do, a flight attendant came to the rescue. "Ma'am, can I help you collect your belongings? I swear this seat you're occupying is not an upgrade. You just can't trust the aisle on these smaller planes. I'll get you an ice pack and keep your wine glass full in flight." She helped return the items to Samantha and strutted to the forward galley. The jet engines hummed.

The flight attendant's voice broke the white noise as she made an announcement over the PA system, requesting all passengers to stow their large electronic devices for taxi and take-off. In a disappointing twist, she added, "Our apologies, but the in-flight WiFi is not working on our aircraft today. We appreciate your patience and thank you for flying with us." With a sense of resignation, Samantha complied with the FAA regulations. She closed her computer, leaving her email in draft form. Mission, unaccomplished.

As Applied in Reality

Smack, Crackle, Pop

Brian shined a light on how to part the gate lice in the terminal and score that coveted seat on a flight to get our journey going. Samantha reveals that it's not all smooth sailing once we're on board the aircraft. Though sometimes a few hard knocks—in the form of unexpected neighbors and unwieldy backpacks—truly shift our perspective and ensure we're seated optimally for our mission. Consider it: smack, crackle, pop.

After that series of three smacks, Samantha's view shifted. I witnessed her brain begin to "crackle" firsthand—not from a concussion, but from the realization that a seating adjustment was in order. No, I wasn't stalking her. Like many of you, I often start recognizing familiar faces while taking the same weekly flights. In a smaller city like Bloomington, that shrinking world becomes even more pronounced, with overlapping circles at hotel bars, restaurants, and client offices. You know those awkward moments—when you make unexpected eye contact, realize you only recognize the person from your flight routine, and quickly divert your gaze. God forbid you start a conversation and have to exchange pleasantries each week. Sometimes, you even start crafting backstories based on accidentally overheard phone calls. Am I the only one who does that?

Anyway, Samantha made her "pop" moment clear after that evening: the regional jet wasn't her personal WeWork. Maybe it was the flight attendant's pointed advice, but Samantha soon favored the window seat, securing her laptop safely against the cabin wall, out of harm's way. On the rare occasions when she opted for an aisle seat, she watched the boarding process like a quarterback reading an incoming defense. She knew when to tuck, when to evade, and when to throw away.

Speaking of quarterbacks—now, my faith forbids idols, but let's just say I'm a huge Tom Brady fan. Random aside, my friends and I had this wild hope that we'd accidentally bump into him at my fortieth birthday in St. Barth's at Nikki Beach's Sunday Funday. It would've been life goals to pop Brut Rosé with the GOAT to ring in the big 4-0, but alas, Brady decided to leave retirement. He missed out, but his record of withstanding hits still stands.

Brady absorbed 546 sacks—the most in NFL history—but each hit brought a lesson. He mastered quick decision-making and impeccable timing, allowing him to throw 649 touchdown passes and earn seven Super Bowl rings. Oh, and let's not forget his GOAT status. Each smack shaped his perspective—helping him learn when to release, when to scramble, and how to maneuver under pressure, all to give his team the best chance at victory.

Backpack wrecking crews exist in the professional world, too. They can stall our progress, or even sack us for losses, if we fail to adapt and learn from the experience.

So how do we use these encounters to better ourselves? First, that metaphorical "smack" from an external force jars us into action. This mental jolt turns the gears in our brains, leading to a "crackle"—the beginnings of new ideas and insights—and ultimately to the "pop," the lightbulb moment that allows us to act. Remember, every smack is followed by a crackle and a pop—it's how we keep our perspective where it needs to be.

It's why Brady's touchdown passes surpass his sacks, and it's why Samantha found peace and productivity on future flights—no more missions unaccomplished. Like Samantha, it took three smacks for my brain to crackle and finally pop to provide the lightbulb moment, the moment that helped me realize where I needed to position myself in my career to achieve my professional goals.

First Smack? "It's the Economy, Stupid"

Samantha's first smack by the backpack crew caught her completely off guard. The laptop bag swung wildly, as if channeling a Miley Cyrus hit—and just like a wrecking ball, it was unaware of the chaos left behind. My first smack was equally devoid of emotion or remorse from the perpetrator. Why? It was the Great Recession. I'm not sure if my brain crackled from that hit or fried from trying to decide if ramen counted as a food group or a financial strategy.

I couldn't tell if it was the ringing in my ears or just some relentless voice in my head, but it kept looping the same pep talk: "C'mon, man. Any job is a good job. You need experience. Don't go thinking you're too good for it."

Lehman Brothers toppled in the fall of 2008 and sent shockwaves through the economy, erasing millions of jobs in a matter of months. Everyone clamored for employment, but opportunities were as scarce as seats on a regional jet. Recruiting efforts halted. Patagonia vests failed as makeshift life jackets.

My opening gig post-law school? Valet boy in Atlanta's posh Buckhead neighborhood. I rubbed elbows with professional athletes, all right, just as they breezed in and out of their vehicles for upscale dinners. It was a slight detour from the original dream. Fun fact: I can still identify a car's make by the specific sound it makes to signal that the seat belt is unfastened.

Given the bleak post-juris doctorate job outlook, I pivoted to a one-year MBA program in Oxford, Mississippi. Familial and friendly ties drew me to Ole Miss, alongside a full fellowship offer. The school also boasted robust relationships with the firms where I sought tax roles, thanks to their highly renowned accounting department. Most importantly, it bought me a year to let the economy recover while Ole Miss footed most of the bill.

Also, relax. I rooted for Eli in both of his Super Bowls. I'm not a bad Rebel. But I did root for Brady in his other pursuits. Apologies, Atlanta friends.

I left Oxford with a law degree, active bar license, MBA, and pending interviews in the Peach State. Not included? A source of income or sense of accomplishment. I was an orca, dorsal fin collapsed, except in my case, it was a popped Vineyard Vines collar lying flat around my neck. Like Samantha's first wrecking crew encounter, I sat aghast and shocked. Did this really just happen?

A generous buddy let me crash on a spare mattress in his guest room in exchange for covering some utilities. I learned to survive on bananas, peanut butter, and protein powder. Okay, that still comprises sixty percent of my diet, but c'mon—have some sympathy. I'd often joked about being dead inside, but that was a humble brag. This was a new low, feeling both crushed and suffocated by the laptop bag that should've been charged with first-degree assault.

My shock from the recession shifted my perspective drastically. My brain churned and even started to crackle. Suddenly, any job in tax seemed as sexy as reprising *Jerry Maguire*—well, unless the duties required me to dress as Lady Liberty and beckon traffic into a tax prep office. I'd nearly ordered the costume from Amazon after parking the last Mercedes during the lunch rush when suddenly, my phone rang.

"Go Gamecocks," said the interviewer, a fellow law school alum. He also "minored" in Lad, just a decade before me.

The offer arrived two weeks later after an office visit. The position? Associate, within KPMG's state and local tax (SALT) group. I'd never studied this particular subject matter, but they exuded confidence that I'd quickly learn. The compensation? $55,000 base, right in line with that of a first-year auditor with only a Bachelor's degree. Ouch.

Despite the pay, deep down I knew: "Any job is a good job. This firm keeps you relevant, and you need a seat on the plane." The acceptance? Verbally, on the spot. I took the job, even if I could only afford J. Roget and Chipotle, the latter just twice a week. The smack hurt, but much like Samantha on the flight, I was eager to get to work. If only I knew more pain was on the way.

Second Smack: The Joneses' Game of Keep Away

Samantha should've seen that second smack coming—the swiveling backpack down the aisle. It was all there if she'd just paid attention. Similarly, after the initial euphoria of full-time employment wore off and the thrill of adding relevant resume bullets faded with a few paychecks, my own "second smack" hit. I, too should've seen it coming, but I had my head down, too focused on finishing school and landing a job to notice what was brewing.

For me, the smack came in the form of creeping resentment—watching my peers pass me by—and the regret over time I'd wasted on choices that now felt unrecoverable. Had I thrown away four years? Backtracked to some point of no return? I wasn't sure if my mind was cracking under the pressure or if those nagging voices had returned, but one thing was clear: I needed a plan. So, I picked up some new survival skills—intra-firm networking and politicking. If I was going to recoup lost time and fast-track my path, it wasn't just about working hard; it was about impressing the right people, too.

Why did that second smack sting so hard? Two fold. One, enrollment in graduate school masked the disparity in quality of life between me and my peers. Two, survival mode kicked in once I moved to Atlanta. When I accepted the offer, I started to re-emerge and began to look around. My college friends had now secured mortgages on primary residences, many taking advantage of the plummeted real estate values and low interest rates. Others sold companies, made millions, and started acquiring vacation homes or investment properties. At minimum, they'd joined a country club. Me? I weighed gas prices for a commute against monthly rental amounts. I subscribed to an email service that alerted me to deeply discounted golf rounds.

The worst part? They presumed my job, which I'd fancified for LinkedIn, paid commensurate with the number of degrees I'd collected. Offers and invites to partake in lavish vacations, social clubs and charity events soon followed. My inability to afford and accept crushed my pride and ego.

Thankfully, predatory credit card companies allowed me to fake a lifestyle quality to my peers, and I shed the debt by taking advantage of bankruptcy laws. Totally kidding. Go ahead and search.

I never envisioned stressing over cocktail tabs, restaurant prices, or rent after earning my JD and MBA, much less after graduating from SMU. Sure, maybe if I lost credit card roulette at Bagatelle or French Laundry, or perhaps if I'd selected a Gramercy brownstone to call home alone, but that wasn't my world. No, I lived with roommates in Atlanta and frequented the SweetWater Brewery's fifteen-dollar fixed-price happy hour. It was incredibly difficult to shake that I somehow commanded less salary firepower with two graduate degrees than I did fresh out of college. Talk about an ROI misfire. The recurring thoughts and resentment resembled that backpack on a swivel.

Don't worry. This isn't a pity party. Those suck, and they never serve good wine or tequila. Still, it was at this moment that my brain started to crackle a bit more. I had to improve my outlook.

I got to work. I showed up early. I left late. There wasn't a task or ask too big or too small I wouldn't offer to tackle. Fortunately, my unorthodox background allowed the SALT practice to use me on a variety of projects—one notable engagement involved tax due diligence. Diligence is the "background check" companies conduct before they merge with a company or acquire a business. It's homework during the deals process.

"Hotty Toddy!" the M&A tax partner exclaimed to open the call, the Ole Miss rallying cry.

My ears perked and head tilted like a golden retriever upon hearing the word "squirrel."

"Indeed. Go Rebs," replied a director within the same practice.

My team provided our analysis and review of whether the company in question complied with state and local tax laws to the M&A tax team and concluded the call. The pair said they'd reach out if they needed our support during any follow-up discussions with the client. With my interest piqued and ears still perked, I went to LinkedIn. My brain started to crackle.

Wayne, the M&A tax partner, boasted three degrees from Ole Miss: his Bachelor's, an MBA, and a JD. Well, wasn't that trio of diplomas quite interesting? He also added an LLM in tax from NYU to his trophy case. LLMs are master of laws degrees. Professor Brant received his LLM from the very same program at NYU. Okay, so Wayne was a genius, too.

Evidently, Wayne left a high-powered New York law firm to form the new practice at KPMG. He was the national lead. Deals and tax? This is what we learned in Brant's classes, the very subject matter that jump-started my pivot down this flight path. My interest crescendoed from piqued to peaked. Could I transfer? Now I really wanted his team to need more SALT support for that diligence project. I waited and waited for that call. I needed an excuse to interject "Hotty Toddy" with Wayne on the line.

The follow-up call never came, but a SALT colleague and good friend of mine knew someone currently working in the M&A tax group, Reid. She introduced us over lunch, and unbeknownst to her, Reid and I would become lifelong friends and permanent ski buddies.

"Well, once Wayne finds out you went to Ole Miss, he's going to transfer you to our group whether you want to or not. So, I'd just make sure this is the move you want to make before y'all meet," Reid informed me.

"You should do it. It just makes so much more sense given your background," my SALT teammate replied.

She was right. And Reid was right. I checked the bios of the team Wayne built; it was littered with Ole Miss alums. Reid set up a lunch and I crash-coursed notes I'd saved from Professor Lad's and Brant's classes. My hope? The conversation would move quickly from my interest in the group to all things Oxford and Ole Miss. I had to make the connection personal.

One week later, Reid, Wayne, and I met for lunch with two other M&A tax practitioners in downtown Atlanta. As I'd hoped, we talked tax and transfer for ten minutes and Ole Miss for the remaining hour and change. Wayne was awesome and I enjoyed the shared camaraderie for the Rebels, but the actual conversation left me a little scared that his opinions of my tax expertise and ability to perform in the group were waning. Had I networked and politicked internally incorrectly? As I sullenly slunk down at my desk in a food coma, my phone rang.

"So when would you like to move over? I already screened your work ethic and product quality before lunch. Frankly, I just needed to make sure I liked you. I've started the transfer process if you're ready." Showtime, sports fans.

"And don't worry, I'm already working on your comp adjustment."

Hell Yes. Damn Right. I was moving up. Reid was right; I knew I trusted that guy. He was also a fan of the Manning family, just of the Peyton variety.

It was time to shed the worn Vineyard Vines—I'd finally graduated to Peter Millar. Sure, I did some schmoozing, but I also worked my ass off for pennies. And I made damn sure that the right people saw that effort at the right time. I also built the relationships that could protect me as I learned the new ropes, and that protective sphere was crucial. I'm lucky I didn't wear it completely thin. The resentment I'd felt towards my peers started to fade, though it never disappeared entirely—one last smack was still waiting for me.

Third Smack: You Suck at This

After Samantha's second smack, she mistakenly thought the worst was over—just a few more passengers to board and she could finally finish that paragraph. Nope. Enter Mr. Kimchi, and suddenly her mission was "unaccomplished." My version of that third smack? Realizing that despite law school, an MBA, and three years of tax work, I was still floundering in Wayne's practice. Alright, maybe "sucking" is a bit much, but honestly, not by far. It was a brutal wake-up call. Just like Samantha, I'd been lulled into a false sense of security—my billable hours and utilization had me wrapped in a cozy little cocoon of competence and job security, but reality had other plans.

After the transfer, even in Atlanta, the move to M&A tax put some Texas swagger back into my step. Or as President George W. Bush famously called it, "walking." Now in the deals space, I could once again quote B-school movies like *Boiler Room*, *Wall Street*, and *American Psycho* without raging jealousy for those actually working in desirable fields.

I also learned the *Wolf of Wall Street* chest-thump song and routinely re-enacted the scene with a few coworker friends. Complete tool move, but no apologies. Yeah, I know. We were still in tax. But M&A tax!

Wayne built an incredible practice with talented individuals. He genuinely cared about his people and shepherded those with affinities for Ole Miss.

Thank God for that. One afternoon, before I deployed on a project that would initiate me into the world of points and status, I sat in his office on a broad diligence call with a client.

The client, a company's head of M&A, asked each advisor on the line to discuss the merits and risks associated with the proposed deal. She needed to confirm that the pros outweighed the cons before recommending the acquisition to the CEO and investment committee. Legal, finance, commercial, operations, environmental, and of course - tax experts all chimed in to give their points of view. She seemed satisfied that the deal was a strategic fit but had some ammunition to renegotiate some deal points to her company's advantage. My mind pondered, crackled even, "How do I land that job?"

I started to ask Wayne about that role when he informed me that a managing director drafted me to help support the tax efforts for a major US chemical company selling off several business units. They were multi-billion-dollar deals, and the client wanted us on-site every week. That's when I began my weekly travel routine. Time for my utilization and airline status to soar.

A quick bit on utilization. Professional services firms rely on their advisors to generate revenue, we're the product. Law firms set billable hours goals for the year. Consulting and advisory firms use a similar mechanism but apply percentages on a weekly basis. For example, if the firm decides that forty hours per week is the target, your billed hours for the week are divided by that number to calculate your utilization. Investment banks? They return 1/1000th of your soul to you after every eighty-hour work week. Slightly tongue in cheek.

High utilization levels earned me a quick, initial promotion. I was a workhorse. High travel frequency quickly got me to the highest tiered airline status and Ambassador level with SPG hotels (RIP). I was now also a points whore. Oh, and the raise? I could now afford Chandon intermittently and occasionally splurge at Hillstone, without even using my points balances. I was head down, and it seemed as though the boarding process was nearing completion. The final wrecking crew culprit? Like I said, my own work product.

Utilization and work ethic elevate you quickly at the early stages. But to receive the more meaningful promotions, the higher-ups need to trust your ability to validate the accuracy of others' work. How do you earn that trust? You produce a clean work product of your own that's error-free.

Make no mistake, I always strived to maintain the right attitude. Key word: strived. People liked working with me. Not only because I put in the hours, but also because I kept that social chair aura about me. Sadly, my work product grade level in tax was B- on the norm and B+ on my best day, and not for lack of effort. Every work hour felt like slogging through a problem on Professor Lad's chalkboard. I went to the directors and managing directors often for help, as though they held office hours. It felt like I needed to study for Professor Lad's and Brant's exams on a daily basis. Once per semester? Fine. But each and every day? The review comments spoke for themselves. Red ink galore. I relived the corporate rendition of the *Game of Thrones* "Red Wedding" scene on loop. And honestly, like Samantha, I should've smelled that smack from a mile away, given the scent of all the red ink bleeding across my deliverables.

"Please Fix," the weapon of choice.

I tried. I really tried to improve each week, to fully "get it." But it didn't click. I was a tax Gronkowski. Needless to say, I did not receive that meaningful promotion. I knew damn well that I didn't deserve it, but I was still pissed.

Why? I knew it wouldn't happen the next year either. I sucked at this. It was time to face the music.

Try the Window Seat

That last smack hurt. It knocked me to the ground, much like Samantha's phone and laptop right before the boarding door closed. I realized that I needed to find something, somewhere where I could excel. But where was that? I'd invested so much time into school and this tax practice. My mind was crackling, but I needed that to stop, I needed the "pop."

A month after the promotion rejection, I found my pace slowing as I walked. I looked to the left and saw my disheveled reflection in a storefront window. Oof, a haircut beckoned. I heard some commotion to my right—two people bickering over imaginary items from a garbage bin and an empty shopping cart they planned to sell the next day to passersby. It was just a few hours before dawn. No, I hadn't descended into crack den residency. I was simply walking back to the hotel from the client's offices in Wilmington. But I did need a shower.

There was no time to mourn my career path. The deal timelines escalated the hours we worked with brute force. Many nights turned into mornings where we simply escaped to the hotel at sunrise to freshen up, change clothes, and return to the office. No, Bank of America, I'm not looking for work. Fortunately, this morning-ish meander would conclude with packing my bags and flying home that afternoon, for nearly the entire weekend. Yes, it was Friday, and sure, we would return on Sunday evening, but I desperately needed a few nights' sleep in my own fucking bed.

My tax colleagues became close friends and confidants. Three of us on the project called Atlanta home, even though we each filed tax returns in eight states due to work travel. A fourth lived in south Florida and she kept us in line, or at least tried to. Nearing peak delirium that fateful Friday, Joe, Arif, Krystel, and I shuffled through TSA and found real estate at the Philadelphia Sky Club.

"Why the hell do we work like this? We aren't saving any lives at our jobs," I posed to the crew, hands planted on my face, eyes peering between my pinkies and ring fingers towards my beer.

"C'mon man, yes, we do. We're business doctors. We're surgeons. We're cutting out the tumors so the rest of the company can heal and grow," Joe retorted with palpable sarcasm. Arif spit his beer higher than an Icelandic geyser.

"There's literally no way anyone actually believes that bullshit line, right? Also, unless you can assist in a medical emergency on the plane, you're not a damn doctor!" I exclaimed. Two history professors next to us donning tweed blazers passed a judgmental gaze our way.

Suddenly, our phones simultaneously vibrated. Push notification – flight delayed, two hours.

"That plane hasn't even left Atlanta for Philly. It's an insult to our intelligence that they think we believe this new departure time is remotely accurate," Joe said. "Assholes."

"I swear, if we don't make it home tonight, I will find a way to get myself on the 'no-fly' list so I don't have to come back here ever again," I interjected.

"I can help with that," chimed Arif, our Bangladeshi teammate who always joked he was on a government watch list because of his religious beliefs. The ensuing laughter eased our moods a bit. I stood up. "I'll fetch us another round. Gotta love self-serve. No judgment. Are we sticking with beer?"

"Can you just put a straw in that bottle of vodka on the counter?" Joe inquired.

"Whoever sits next to you tonight is going to earn thousands of extra bonus miles," Krystel said.

The scene was a familiar occurrence. We mingled in and out of conversations with each other and others on our phones before we boarded the flight four hours later. Joe was right again.

Arif was my seat neighbor that evening. We were both upgraded, so we turned left as we boarded the Boeing 757. It was 2012, and Delta had yet to retrofit all the birds they inherited in the merger with Northwest Airlines. Ash trays still resided in the center consoles. The seat pockets sagged like the elastic waistband on a thirty-year-old pair of cotton gym shorts. The plane lacked internet, which was actually welcome that evening, but that didn't stop one client email from landing in my inbox on my phone before the boarding door shut.

"I ... don't understand this question," I said, agitated knowing this would lead to weekend work.

"Brandon, c'mon. We went over this on Tuesday," Arif replied after reading my screen.

"I give up, dude. This deal doesn't even make any logical sense."

Arif pushed, "The deal? What do you mean?"

The flight attendant popped by. "Would either of you like a drink before takeoff?"

"Bleach, on the rocks," I said. Before I could apologize, she chuckled and said, "Wow. Dark. Very dark. I like it. Y'all are going to be fun tonight. Thank you both for your Diamond status. So sadly, we're all out of bleach but we do have a Chardonnay, or a quasi-decent Pinot Noir?"

"Pinot," Arif and I exclaimed in unison before I returned to his question.

"I mean, this deal sucks. They carve out this business unit and claim they want to sell to financial buyers. Private equity firms don't just have rosters or benches full of operators to come in and run the day-to-day. They're mechanically packaging the separated business as though some other conglomerate will

46

come in and fold it into their existing operations but marketing it towards buyers with no corporate infrastructure. They didn't stand-up any operations so the company could run independently, and they excluded all the key talent because they wanted to keep it. It's evident by the people we're dealing with daily that the underperformers are moving to the divested company. Also, they excluded operations in some of the emerging markets where the real growth opportunities lie for this business. I'll shut up, but I would bet this thing implodes and short circuits a year after the sale. It's going to–"

"Can I use the b-word?" Arif asked.

"No," I laughed. "You still can't say bomb on an airplane, even if you mean it related to the deal's success," I whispered.

"But you said you wanted to be on the 'no fly' list."

"Touche." We clinked our glasses as the plane headed towards the runway.

The plane took flight at roughly 10:12 p.m. We might have landed before midnight, but my arrival at home technically occurred on Saturday morning. Entire weekend, my ass. I started to prioritize the personal chores I needed to complete between sips of wine when Arif prodded my shoulder and motioned for me to remove my headphones.

"Honest question, why do you stay in tax? You do know people get paid to evaluate all the things you mentioned earlier, right? They probably deliver the news less bluntly, but that's what they look at and examine every day. You could do that for several years and then run the M&A show at a company. That's what you should do, man. That plays to your strengths. This life, tax, it's not for you. I can tell you're not dumb. You're smart, but when I look at your work prod–"

"Yeah, I know, let's not relive it," I interrupted and smirked. I recalled the diligence call with Wayne where I wanted to inquire about that role. That's where I actually wanted to end up. "I guess I just thought I needed to use my law degree somehow to justify its price tag. And what? I just magically go to McKinsey or Bain or BCG?"

"I'm pretty sure not getting promoted beyond senior associate at age thirty is a terrible use of your law degree, too. Also, we have a group that does this now. It's a bit new, but you should really look into it. You have legitimate M&A experience. They will value that a lot."

My brain started to crackle again, maybe due to the altitude and unlimited Pinot Noir, but more so as I thought through the next pivot. Finally, "pop!" It was okay that I wasn't a tax guru after all. There were other areas within the deals world where I could play to my strengths, both academically and practically. I wasn't wasting my education. I wasn't stupid. Well, hopefully.

Arif was right. After our talk, the lightbulb went off—somewhere around thirty thousand feet. Just like Samantha after her third smack, staying in tax felt like trying to force that regional jet into a WeWork station. And to find it, I needed to transfer to this group Arif mentioned.

At a weekend cookout, some Ole Miss friends—a couple who knew I was itching to get out of my current work situation—decided to introduce me to someone who "also worked at KPMG." Don't get me wrong, I love them, but connecting Big 4 folks is usually a waste of time. With thousands of employees worldwide, the odds of knowing anyone outside your own little bubble are pretty much zero. Except this time it wasn't a waste. Of course, I didn't know Justin. But ten minutes in, I found out he was in M&A strategic services, the group Arif suggested. Justin and I are still buddies, and his first introduction for me in the practice group? A fine gentleman who'd made the same leap from tax years before, for the same reasons as me. What were the odds?

As I met more people and got deeper into conversations about the work, my excitement grew. This was exactly the kind of experience I needed if I was going to earn that role I'd overheard on Wayne's call—the head of M&A. After I received the offer, I had to tell Wayne. That sucked.

He reluctantly approved my transfer and let me move to the window seat. It was for honorable reasons; he wanted to make sure I was cared for, and he probably held legitimate doubts regarding my ability to stay employed given the quality of my tax deliverables, but he did it anyway. He still roots for me.

The first comments I received post-transfer still gave "red wedding" vibes. However, a stark and important difference arose in the onslaught of edits. It was all formatting related. The content itself was spot on. I'd found my niche and no longer looked like an idiot at work, albeit after a few courses in PowerPoint. And that was less of a smack, more of a gentle prod. Before long? I was delving out the comments myself.

It took three hard smacks to get me in the door at KPMG, into deals, and into a practice where I could actually obtain useful skills for my long-term career. It sucks to get punched. I hated being broke and feeling embarrassed about it. I hated sucking at my job despite the crazy hours and genuine effort. I hated disappointing Wayne after he took a chance on me. But when I faced the music and let the gears in my brain crackle—after clearing concussion protocols, I finally got to the "pop." Instead of trying to force my degrees and ego into one line of work, I found the window seat that was best for me. My career didn't have to conclude as "mission unaccomplished."

Most importantly, the "pop" shifted my perspective. Now, I was zeroing in on an outcome—the M&A lead role—and figuring out exactly what experience I needed to get there, instead of dwelling on my circumstances. Sounds perfect, but we all know it's not. Even when you love your job and feel confident in your path, you still face thunderstorms. We need strength and endurance to handle the storms that threaten to derail our plans and our focus on the end game. How do we build that?

Lots of pharmaceuticals. No. Like anything else, it takes fuel to keep us from running out of gas and staying on course. And right on schedule, the overhead Tetris flunkee steps in to remind us of this very lesson. So, keep your ice pack handy— it's time to shift our focus from the boarding lane to the overhead bin.

Habit 3: The Overhead Tetris Flunkee

Overhead Tetris Flunkee (*noun*): These are specimens renowned for a striking disregard for the laws of physics and the patience of crew members and fellow passengers. Key habits to note include:

- Bin Shoehorning: Leaves carry-on bag hanging conspicuously over the edges of the overhead bin. These passengers ignore the obvious fact that the bin will not close and nonchalantly stroll to their seat. Believe the laws of physics will somehow bend to accommodate their disregard for common sense or courtesy.
- Expecting Supercalifragilisticexpialidocious: Harbors a peculiar belief that flight attendants possess the magical prowess of Mary Poppins. Expects these diligent professionals to transform their luggage into compact marvels so the bins close with ease.
- Salmoning: When bags are moved behind one's seat to readjust and fit properly in a bin, shifts blame to the flight attendant for placing the bag behind his or her seat. Creates a blockade like a persistent beaver during the exit process, forcing others to pay the price for their own mistakes.

The Fix: You Want to... But Probably Shouldn't

Spot a passenger who places a bag shamelessly hanging beyond the bin's limits. Glance back to confirm the guilty party takes a seat. Turn to the nearest flight attendant, discreetly pluck the offending bag from the bin, pretend it's your own, and request to check it to your own final destination, which is likely different from the bag's rightful owner.

As Seen in the Overhead Bin

Everyone loves a flight delay.

Said no one ever. Okay, not true. I hope for them routinely given I'm often running late to catch my flights. Naturally, that's when they fantastically depart ahead of schedule. And without me.

Not all delays are created equal. Sometimes the holdup is an isolated event—tardy in-bound aircrafts, maintenance issues, or crewless equipment cause these delays. But what happens when there's an error with the air traffic control tower or lingering, severe weather? It's what I call a "Gatequake." Imagine the mass collision of Black Friday shoppers at Walmart, a horde of angry Disney World-goers stuck in the queue of a closed ride, and a mob of businesspersons waiting impatiently at the hostess stand for their unready table at Nobu. For good measure, add in a dash of linguistic bewilderment, where at least five percent of the people in the crowd need assistance but speak a foreign language that nobody tasked with providing answers or guidance is able to translate. Thank heavens for loud, slower English. Did I mention all of this takes place in a confined area behind locked doors with armed guards? With good reason, Dante refused to mention this final layer of hell beyond the ninth circle.

On a muggy August afternoon, I experienced a Gatequake that registered north of a Dante "nine" on the "gridlock" scale. The air traffic control tower at Dallas-Fort Worth (DFW) experienced a fire in the morning that rerouted planes from 10:00 a.m. until just before noon. After personnel rectified that situation, severe storms that included tornadoes gathered and hovered around the airport from 1:30 p.m. until 3:30 p.m. All in all, the events negatively impacted nearly nine hundred flights. If the average flight load was 150 passengers, you can imagine the tenor of the terminals that afternoon.

I expected a lengthy delay for my 5:45 p.m. flight to Kansas City, but the airline's app indicated my flight would depart on time, so I trekked to the airport. As I neared the airport just under an hour before departure, I received a text. Delay? Nope, just a gate change. The departure gate alerted me that my flight would now leave from Terminal C. C as in careworn. Word of the day.

Careworn, or neglected, terminals that were last renovated before Los Del Rio inflicted the "Macarena" on civilization aren't uncommon. At DFW, that's C. That blistering day, it also appeared the HVAC unit gave out. My hopes that the crushing heat I felt at the entrance would dissipate once I moved beyond security and away from the sliding doors fell entirely flat. I cleared through TSA and noticed a terminal thermostat that read eighty-three degrees. "Miserable," I thought as I received another push notification: this time the first flight delay, one hour. "Uh oh. Better hit the Admirals Club and see what's going on here."

The C terminal Admirals Club befits the concourse it inhabits. If it were a sound, it would be a sigh. The air conditioning problems continued well into the club's confines that afternoon. Fortunately, I knew of a cubicle in the business center area that nestled right below an air vent. On most days, it resembled sitting below a frosty close talker. Unfortunately, that day it was more like someone who'd eaten an Altoid a few hours ago, but it was still better than nothing.

Thanks to the flowing air, I could at least focus on the task at hand. I propped open my laptop and immediately opened two browser tabs. I scanned FlightAware to determine the current location of my scheduled flight's aircraft. It had diverted to Wichita and still sat on the tarmac. Time spent in Wichita? Nearly two hours. Eek. My phone buzzed. The airline extended my delay to two and a half hours. "This isn't good."

I searched the airline's website to uncover the remaining flights to Kansas City. Good news, there was a 7:15 p.m. flight. Even better? That aircraft was en route and would arrive at Gate C24 in forty-five minutes. By jove, it was on time.

I noticed the struggling air conditioning started to impact my mood. As sweat threatened to dot my shirt like a Georges Seurat painting, the volume of a nearby conversation irked me to the brink of making a shushing noise. I refrained, turned up the volume of the Kygo album playing in my headphones and refilled a glass of ice water to calm myself down.

I sat back down and finished my research. The good news I'd uncovered about the flight came with some crucial bad news. No available seats. However, given the unfolding gatequake, a passenger was bound to miss their connection. I just needed my name on the standby list.

I humbly sauntered to the lounge's concierge desk with roughly a tablespoon of hope that I would secure a seat. It was noticeably hotter here without direct access to the air vent. And that's where I first stumbled upon Mr. and Mrs. Banks. They were a youngish couple, in their late 30s or early 40s. Amidst the ironic blaring of Kygo's "Freeze" in my ears, I learned they urgently needed to get home after their escapades in Key West. The flight path matched their odor. Downwind from the couple, I smelled lingering sunscreen and the faint scent of a mango White Claw. They both sported Kansas City Chiefs t-shirts and Mr. Banks's voice currently resonated at volumes typically reserved for crucial third-down plays in tightly contested playoff games.

"Listen ma'am. We got little to no sleep last night because we wanted to enjoy our last night of vacation. Is that a crime? No, not the last time I checked. Key West held up its end of the bargain. You haven't. There weren't any issues with our flights until we landed here in Dallas. Do you realize that when we get home, we will have to drive another hour and a half before we can reach our bed? Your airline thought it was appropriate to schedule a thirty-minute connection for us, and we missed that flight. They rebooked us with a three-hour connection, and now that flight is nowhere in sight. We need you to put us on the 7:15 and let us in the club. It is hot as hell in the terminal and there's nowhere to sit. You're telling me you can't sell us a couple of day passes so we can lay down for a bit? Most places are happy to take our money," Mr. Shane Banks clamored as sweat dripped down his forehead. His wife stood faithfully by his side and repeated, "Yeah, you tell her, Shane," throughout the exchange.

"Great, they want on my flight," I sighed before I noticed their luggage. The bags themselves were ordinary rollerboards, but the sight today was anything but. The Banks had released the expansion compartments. Despite this, the bags' zippers only came within two inches of each other. Zip ties clasped and gripped with all their might to hold everything together. It looked like someone wore summer body jeans for Thanksgiving dinner instead of stretchy pants. Suddenly, another push notification: three hours and fifteen minutes delayed. Now I was really sweating. My nerves rose sharply. I needed my name on the list to know my rank and chances. "These two cannot take my seat," I thought before tuning back into the unfolding mess.

"Sir, I understand you're frustrated but, as you can see, we are at full capacity. There's nowhere to sit in here, much less lie down. We unfortunately don't control building maintenance at the airport so I can't adjust the temperature. We are all hot. As for your flight, I can't rebook you. You'll have to go to C26. We're experiencing a lot of delays here today due to the air traffic control fire earlier and because of the severe weather that hit the area," the agent sternly but politely replied to Shane.

I'd spotted three open cubicles near me and even a few empty coves in the club. The concierge probably knew this fact, but the Banks' egos and tempers were far too large to comfortably fit in the space that day, much like the items in their suitcases. "Where did they find zip ties in Key West? On second thought, I don't want to know," I mused and started eavesdropping once again.

"Ma'am, take your happy ass downstairs and take a look outside. There isn't a cloud in the sky. It hasn't rained in over an hour! And you're going to blame this delay on the weather? What's the point of having that computer in front of you if you can't book us seats? Sounds like excuses. Evidently, I need to talk to someone way above you for solutions," Shane protested.

"Karen's a man, a meteorologist and wants to speak to the manager." Shit, I'd blurted it aloud.

"What did you say?" He replied as he turned towards me. I quickly waved my hand, shook my head and pointed down at my phone screen. Then made the "sorry" face to the agents.

"Right. You stay out of this... 'Lulu' boy," he retorted. Mizzen + Main! I was wearing Mizzen + Main.

Shane again demanded seats. Naturally, she couldn't deliver. He then demanded her name and employee number, vowing to report her alleged misconduct to some higher-up. She obliged and provided him the 1-800 number for customer service before again directing him to gate C26 for further assistance.

The Banks stormed off, and I swore I heard the wheels on their bags wince in pain.

"Having a fun day?" I asked as I approached the desk. They both laughed and asked how they could assist me. "Sorry if I made that worse earlier."

Attempting genuine self-deprecation, I began, "So... I have a completely unreasonable and obnoxiously trivial request. I was hoping I could get listed standby for this 7:15 p.m. flight to Kansas City because it is taking off earlier than my flight that was scheduled for 5:45. I know there's likely no shot of me making it but any chance? You can load me underneath."

"Let me see." The agent typed away, and then grinned, saying, "Okay, you'll need to go down to gate C19. They are changing gates and that's where that flight will take off, and I actually think you will make the flight due to some inbound delays. But you do need to be at the gate to accept the seat confirmation. Just know your upgrade doesn't transfer, so be prepared for a middle seat."

"On a sixty-two minute flight? I think I can muster the sacrifice," I said and held my right hand to my heart, tapping my iPhone against my chest.

"You'd be surprised," the agent next to him responded.

I exited the club to make my way down to C19. The concourse was terrifying. In a war of first-world problems, it felt like storming the beaches of Normandy. Except instead of facing Nazis and fighting for something actually important like western civilization, I faced the kingdom of angry couponers and needed to grab my Starbucks mobile order before the ice melted and watered down my drink. I arrived at C19 and searched for a discreet spot to watch the monitor for my stand-by status. As I waited, another notification flashed on my phone screen—a daunting four-and-a-half-hour delay for my original flight. "I have to get on this bird," I muttered to myself.

Twenty painstaking minutes passed before I heard, "Mr. Blewett, please approach the podium for your boarding pass." Hallelujah! I crawled through the gate lice to fetch my ticket.

Suddenly, the Banks re-entered the chat. "Superb, they made it on this flight."

The pair's bags steamrolled the uncovered toes in the crowd on their way to the front of the boarding area, sparking angry echoes of "hey" in the gate house. The Banks still believed their inconveniences outweighed those of everyone else at the airport, including families with frustrated toddlers and people seated in wheelchairs. The gate agent abruptly stopped them.

Mr. Banks indignantly interjected, "Sir, you don't know what we've been through thanks to your airline. We're just going to board first quietly so we can get situated on this flight and go home."

"Glad you'll make it home like many of your fellow passengers, but we have to board according to the groups assigned on your boarding passes. Group seven will be called in numerical order," the agent replied.

I mentally high-fived the agent.

A small part of me wanted to witness a Ben Stiller moment from *Meet the Parents* and watch the Banks duo anxiously wait for the gate agent to call the final zone. However, much more of me wanted to sit in functioning air conditioning and find room overhead for my bag. I boarded with my designated zone and settled into my middle exit-row seat. The arctic air created a holy grail of comfort on a flight that promised me time to shower and sleep before my morning meetings. Yes, I'd admittedly be the first torch extinguished on a season of *Survivor*.

Flight attendants made futile pleas for passengers not to stack their larger luggage in the overhead bins like books, "Please don't turn your bags on their sides. This aircraft is not equipped with oversized bins. We'd prefer not to incur a delay by checking additional bags."

The Banks suddenly appeared. Naturally, they audaciously jumped the boarding order. Then they looked my way.

"No, please God. I'm so sorry for those thoughts I had earlier! No. They're walking in my direction," I ensured the thoughts remained internal this time.

Mrs. Banks shot me a disdainful look and declared that I was occupying her seat. Retrieving the phone from my pocket, I pulled up my boarding pass to make sure I was in the right spot.

Meanwhile, Mr. Banks struggled to arrange their luggage to fit in the overhead compartment across the aisle. Shocker. Ignoring the flight attendant, he left them protruding several inches into the cabin. He joined his wife in the intense stare down, leaned in and delivered an ultimatum. "Look dude, you're in my wife's seat. We're already delayed enough. Go sit where you were assigned," he proclaimed.

I refrained from channeling my inner Logan Roy and snapping, "Fuck off!" Instead, I silently displayed my screen to Shane and revealed my seat assignment: 13E, the very seat I occupied. Right on cue, a flight attendant approached, offering assistance.

"Alrighty, what do we have going on here?" she asked. "Let's not go viral!" The Banks wasted no time explaining that I was occupying one of their seats and handed their boarding passes to the flight attendant, who swiftly examined them and identified the issue.

"Alrighty! So y'all were assigned 13E and F on your Key West to DFW flight, as shown on these boarding passes," she clarified, returning the first set of passes to Mrs. Banks. "For this flight, you were assigned 10B and C," and handed back the second pair of tickets for this segment.

"Well, what are we supposed to do now that our bags are back here? There's no space above our seats," both Banks shrilled.

"Well, in situations like this, passengers typically return to their assigned seats. This isn't musical chairs, darling, so I recommend locating row ten. You can retrieve your bags once we land."

"Alright, everyone back up," Shane barked, moving his arms in a pushing motion. "This airline seems incapable of making anything straightforward. We need to get to row ten."

Three whole rows. Evidently, it was the Banks' apocalypse now. "The horror."

Despite his demands, passengers disregarded the mandate and navigated around the couple. The poor aisle passengers in rows eleven and twelve winced as their faces collided with bags and bellies while the Banks fought against the current like salmon. The wrecking crew struck again. Finally, the Banks settled into their seats in row ten.

As the boarding process neared its end, the flight attendants diligently monitored the overhead storage, engaging in hushed phone conversations to discuss available bin space for the remaining passengers. They closed those bins at maximum capacity. When necessary, they kindly asked passengers if smaller bags belonged to them, requesting that passengers store items under their seats to create more room. As they rearranged bags to ensure the compartment doors would securely latch, the satisfying sound of clicks echoed through the cabin like crickets on a summer night. The sounds signaled a nearing departure. However, the clicking abruptly ceased when they reached row thirteen. I glanced up to confirm the culprits.

The Banks' luggage protruded like a golden retriever stuck mid-jump onto the kitchen counter, if you omitted all cuteness and endearment from the situation. The flight attendant inquired if the bags belonged to anyone in the immediate area.

"While I like to think of myself as magical, I'm afraid I'm not Mary Poppins and can't make these bags fit in this bin."

No response.

"I see. I guess these bags are even more magical than myself!" Still, no response.

My gaze and index finger discreetly gestured towards row ten. The flight attendant responded with a facial expression that confirmed she understood and subsequently rolled her eyes. She summoned her colleague, and together they relocated the Banks' bags towards the back of the plane.

Seventeen agonizing minutes ticked by, and my worries grew as I heard the failed attempts at closing the bin. It sounded like the constant slamming of a car door with the lock jammed. I feared a compounded delay due to the complex logistics of scheduling takeoff times during gatequakes. I nearly started to sweat when I joyously heard that final click as the flight attendant grabbed Mr. Banks' boarding pass from his right hand and ushered a bag to the front of the plane. Finally, I heard the thud of the boarding door. We were ready for departure.

I chuckled under my breath as I observed Shane's outrage when the flight attendant returned his boarding pass and informed him that she checked one bag and placed the other at the back of the plane. "Stupid hobbitses," I grinned sinisterly like Gollum from *Lord of the Rings*.

The airline's text system, oblivious to the fact that they rebooked me on a different flight, still found it necessary to send me a push notification that my original flight was officially canceled. "Thank you, Lord," I thought to myself. I heard the ding notifying us we were cleared for takeoff before the jets roared us airborne.

Sixty-two minutes later, we touched down in Kansas City and "swiftly" taxied towards our designated gate. Pun intended. When the seatbelt sign switched off, the Banks huffed and puffed in their upstream journey to the rear of the plane. They frantically urged passengers to let them pass; however, their pleas fell on deaf ears. Passengers continued to disembark row by row.

"Shane, we're going to be the last ones off the plane and we still have to go to baggage claim now," Mrs. Banks moaned as they moved slowly towards the back of the plane like tranquilized salmon. "I have to be at work at 7:30 a.m. tomorrow, Shane!"

Twenty-eight minutes later, the Banks finally deplaned, last on board and followed only by the flight's crew. Reuters allegedly reported that they were the last passengers aboard that flight to reach their beds that evening.

As Applied in Reality

Anticipating the Travel Delay

Look, I get it. Brian and Samantha were sympathetic characters—rootable, even. If you're not a complete tool, you were probably glad to see them eventually get where they needed to go. It's easy enough to draw some warm, fuzzy lesson from their circumstances turning around.

But the Banks? What are we supposed to take away from their saga? Not to get blitzed on Duval Street before a marathon of cross-country flights and scream at the gate agents because we're hungover? Honestly, yeah. That's actually a pretty solid takeaway if you want to get where you're headed—and maybe not finish dead last.

I won't lie. The airport deserved a "Razzy" for its performance that day. It almost seemed cursed—someone definitely uttered "Macbeth" backstage that morning. And if you read my desperate chats with the airline's outsourced help desk, you might've lumped me in with the Banks. I'm probably on some watchlist in whatever country fields those customer support requests. Faults laid bare for readers, I still knew how to act at the airport if I had any shot at grabbing a seat on the flight to Kansas City. So why did I react to the chaos differently than the Banks?

My mom would be disappointed to hear it wasn't those etiquette classes we took in early middle school. No, the difference was the Banks were running on fumes, while I had an air vent, some ice water, and Kygo and Zac Brown's "Someday" on repeat—enough that it made my Spotify Wrapped for the fourth year in a row. In short, I had fuel in the tank. That's what got me through the gatequake and to Kansas City right on schedule.

We've all been there—caught in a gatequake, running on empty, acting out of pure exhaustion. Maybe the Banks' behavior bothers you because, deep down, you've acted in a similar manner. No judgment here—I've been there, too. We've all run on the same level of "E" our moms did when chauffeuring us between practices. We're sleep-deprived, stressed, maybe even a little hungover, and suddenly there are issues with our itineraries. The Banks' reactions weren't completely without reason—they just weren't the right ones.

But here's the thing: the Banks knew there was a chance of a delay thanks to the airline's notification. They could've planned better—switched flights, gotten a decent night's sleep, or at least taken steps to have some fuel reserves. Instead, they pushed ahead, running on empty, and ended up making things worse—for themselves and everyone else. They wound up home dead last, trailing behind all the other passengers who found a way to navigate the chaos without self-destructing.

Sweltering Terminals in the Workplace

The popularity of workplace memes, especially the "Everything is Fine" dog surrounded by flames, speaks volumes about how often we face our own professional gatequakes. It's not uncommon to want to unload on clients, colleagues, or opposing counsel just like Mr. Banks did in the Admirals Club. But the brief catharsis would likely fade the moment a 4 p.m. Friday meeting invite from HR hits your inbox.

How do we maintain perspective, remembering the fleeting nature of the sweltering terminal and focusing on the ultimate goal of getting home? What fuels us in our professional journeys? Motivation. It's what keeps our tank full. It's the air vent, the ice water, the tunes – and sometimes a concourse binge.

Binge watch, that is. My guilty pleasure is HGTV. My favorite shows are *Hometown* and *Love It or List It*. I'd gladly share a "Hotty Toddy" chant and a bottle of wine with the Napiers. I'd love to copy and paste Hilary Farr's wit and perfectly delivered sarcasm into my own DNA. On both shows, they take poorly designed and dilapidated properties and transform them into functional and aesthetically pleasing homes. They do this amid gatequakes featuring thunderstorms, hot terminals, and outdated infrastructure, dealing with mold, load-bearing walls, and unsound foundations.

I'd certainly watch it, but *Burning Down the House* wouldn't last more than a few episodes once the arson charges kicked in. Pesky rules. On their shows, neither Hilary nor the Napiers engage in Banks-like behavior. While I sometimes wish they would, they don't berate homeowners, chastise contractors, or pour gasoline on properties more aptly labeled dumpster fires. They see the forest through the trees and find the best design ideas to fit the client's needs. What fuels them through the gatequakes. Ben Napier finds stress relief in woodworking, creating tangible pieces that keep him grounded. His wife Erin often sketches to help visualize ideas, turning stress into creativity. Hilary recharges through travel and time with her dogs. All of these are fuel sources to help maintain perspective amid renovation chaos. It ensures they all see the big picture, the completed project.

Finding the Air Vent

I didn't figure this out early on. Law school and my tax career devolved into gatequakes at times. Like the Banks' flight issues, my career trajectory infuriated me, and I behaved just as poorly on occasion. Thankfully, those cringe moments only haunt me about five nights a year now. Thank God for therapy—and Ambien.

I held high hopes that consulting would be different, but I still needed to recalibrate. The travel, hours, and client demands weren't going anywhere. I needed something to propel me through the gatequakes and keep my eyes on the prize: acquiring the skills to be the M&A lead one day. And that's when I met my dear friend Adderall.

My first cardiac arrest occurred at the age of twenty-eight. No, no. That didn't happen. Though tempting, I typically strayed from vices that worsened my insomnia. Instead, I found my fuel in "gainz" and angel wings—fitness and faith.

Fitness is my ultimate stress reliever. Lifting weights, sprints, circuits—they help me blow off steam and remind me to take care of my body, which keeps my mind right. It's also a tangible reminder that progress is ongoing—you don't get fit once and call it a lifetime achievement. Just like our careers, staying in shape is about constant work and adapting to the next challenge. It's a cycle that keeps the long-term goal in focus and provides near-term fuel, especially when life throws gatequakes at you. It's how I avoid those Banks-level meltdowns—most of the time, at least.

And then there's faith. Don't worry, I'm not about to preach the prosperity gospel here. Though the *Righteous Gemstones* air fleet would help us dodge pesky strangers. Faith, for me, is a reminder that I'm not God, nor am I in full control—and that's probably good news for everyone, even if the latter portion often irritates me. If my plan fails, it doesn't mean there isn't a bigger one in play, one where I might still play a significant role. That's comforting and motivating when things don't go as scripted. Is it always easy to embrace? Hell no. Pun intended.

So how did these fuel sources hold up when I transitioned into management consulting?

Leaving Key West Ain't No Beach

Mr. Banks started his tirade at the Admirals Club with an interesting fact: his flight from Key West to Dallas was fine. Key West lived up to their part of the bargain. He seemed to think that because of that, everything else would go smoothly. He had enough fuel to get through if things stayed on course.

The transfer to consulting initially went according to plan. I was the Banks on their first segment, though in noticeably better attire, and bound for locations with far fewer street daiquiris and less unwanted nudity.

That doesn't mean it was a breeze. There were some doozy projects, but I saw that those exposed me to valuable subject matters and situation rooms. Besides, there was something fun about the shared struggle of consulting life, like being in on an inside joke. All the meme accounts on social? They made sense. It was almost like a club. And honestly, I was having fun. It helped that I finally didn't suck at work. Promotions came quickly. The money wasn't bad either.

I re-engaged with yesteryear's peers without fear that my breath reeked of failure. I'd even graduated to the occasional Moët or Veuve and learned the value of four-way stretch work attire. Baggage upgrades followed. In fact, people with cheap luggage were now dead "Tumi."

My comedy side-gig shockingly failed.

I didn't really attempt comedy. My early career dreams and tax deliverables were jokes enough on their own. In consulting, though, I still worked with some characters. Yours truly not excepted, the cast also included Rich. Initially, we were quite skeptical of each other.

"I thought you were a complete tool when I first met you," we said in unison. "Jinx."

"Ha. It was the vest, wasn't it?" I asked.

"Ummm sure, and maybe that stupid strap holding your sunglasses around your neck, the matching monogrammed bags, oh, and your shirt's sleeves rolled back just enough to showcase a very underwhelming watch choice," he replied.

"Oh wow, sorry it wasn't shiny enough or gold. I guess I should've left my shirt unbuttoned just one more like yours so that everybody could bask in awe at that stunning chain you wore during your *Jersey Shore* audition. Can I get a fist pump? Jaeger bombs, anyone?"

The bromance wrote itself shortly thereafter. We were Zack Morris and AC Slater from *Saved by the Bell*, now navigating the consulting years. Rich and I worked together on multiple transactions, successfully navigating dicey deals and growing quite adept at handling tense situations. Partners loved pairing us together. They understood that if they let us lift in the mornings and exert cardio in the evenings, we'd work like mules and wouldn't complain. We were their handy *Gremlins* if you exposed us to whey protein after midnight.

After the firm tragically separated us for a year, Rich and I found ourselves on the dreaded "beach list." The list is a menu of consultants not staffed on active engagements, needing a new assignment. The name hilariously presumed we had lulls between projects long enough for elongated vacations rather than a one-way flight to Tulum. From Texas.

Soon enough, staffing scooped us both up again, and it would put to the test everything I'd learned about keeping my fuel levels where they needed to be. Up until now, everything about the transfer had gone just as planned, but now I'd arrived in Dallas.

A Corporate "Gatequake"

"It's just a holding tank. I promise," Ray informed us.

Ruh roh. That doesn't sound good.

It wasn't. We found ourselves in the corporate rendition of the Terminal C "gatequake." Rich and I typically sought projects run by Ray, the partner for this "holding tank" project. He was usually one of our favorites.

The nice thing about working in deals is that the project timelines are generally finite and shorter than those in other consulting practices. Even if the client is demanding or a partner leans heavily on comments, there's an element of survivability thanks to the temporariness of the work. Plus, it helped knowing that the skills I learned with each deal gave me the experience to eventually call my own M&A shots.

Admittedly, the deal market was slower at this point in time, so Rich and I couldn't be picky. The project was deal "adjacent." Oof. The client planned to sell three business units and planned for a mega-merger upon completion of the divestitures. They needed financial statements for the carved-out businesses to make this all happen, so they hired a third-party army of accountants to create them. The team was way behind and over budget. The mandate for me and Rich? Make the accountants work faster and rein in their expenses.

Sounds simple, except the timeline here was indefinite. It could take years to receive regulatory approvals. Years? Our longest engagements were usually around three to six months. Moreover, accountants loathe project management, more so than lawyers. Pre-arrival, the pocket-protector army hated us. They informed the client that the only way to expedite the project and cut costs was to dump all of their administrative and office management duties on me and Rich. The client obliged. We were now czars of the clerical grind. "For the motherland!"

Our duties offended menial labor if you likened the two, and neither Rich nor I ever felt above grunt work. It was like demo day with Hilary or the Napiers. All projects require it now and then. Sometimes it's even a welcome reprieve when your mental muscles need a rest. But there's a difference between tedious work and conscripted, futile ditch digging. Stalin would have envied these gulags.

Okay, gulags in a purely first-world sense. We worked from a largely abandoned corporate campus in a back building that was nearly uninhabited. At the front entrances were cubicles last used in 1996. If you followed the flickering hallway lights to the back of the building, you'd find us in the converted warehouse space across from the loading docks. Here, they crafted a makeshift office setting with zero windows, stocked with clearance furniture from IKEA that was probably missing parts.

With palpable condescension, the accounting KGB demanded we replenish snacks, stock office supplies, repair small appliances, organize seating charts, and book conference rooms. Oftentimes, they'd explicitly write out their requests only to backtrack once we completed the task. I meant ranch flavored! Red markers, not black! I wanted the stand-up desk! I said three-hole punch paper! Not the boardroom! Fill in the ditch, dig it up again. Rinse and repeat.

By month three, Rich and I were both jacked and shredded. Our GNC points balances rivaled our airline and hotel accounts. Fuel me up, baby.

Cue month six. Rich and I led a series of trash-side TED talks. Why? The fixed asset team incorrectly placed pizza boxes with scraps in the recycling bin. Waste management wouldn't empty the bin due to the contents. Rodents then found their way into the workspace. Naturally, it was our fault. Labels on bin lids weren't conspicuous enough. We made flyers in Microsoft Paint, plastered them to walls, and hosted fireside chats after we orchestrated the mass murder of Mickey Mouse's entire family. We earned ourselves eight packs, and a lifetime ban from Disney properties.

Despite the environment, Rich and I started each week the same. We greeted one another at the airport, dual fist-bumped, and said, "This will be the week it gets better. Another deal will hit and we can leave here."

It never did, on either account. The worst part? We gained no valuable skills and there appeared to be no end in sight. It was a wasteland, literally and figuratively.

Approaching the Admirals Club Concierge

It was month nine when we received an email request to replace the water jug, fix the coffee machine, and somehow boost internet speed. It came from a summer intern, a college sophomore. She punctuated each request with six question marks and two exclamation points.

"Dude, I legit can't do this indefinitely," Rich said. "My brain is rotting. Do they want me to put tinfoil on my head and crawl on the roof to see if we get a better connection? I'll jump."

"Fermenting. Our brains will be a fine wine when the zombies finally surface in this hellscape. And I'll climb up there with you, with a storm rod," I mused. Neither of us laughed.

Rich and I were running on fumes that morning, thanks to a few too many rounds of sake at the sushi joint by our hotel the night before. We'd struck up a rapport with the bartender, who rewarded our grumbling with generous pours. Missing our gym session only added to the fog of guilt that hung over us, making the day's requests feel even more exasperating. "Yeah, I'm gonna replace the water jug then email Ray. There has to be another project. Any," I said.

I started to type, only to realize I felt exactly like Mr. Banks at the Admirals Club—except I was pleading with Ray instead of the concierge. Was I fueled up enough to handle this properly, or was I standing on the brink of my own meltdown?

Subject: Project and staffing touch base

Hi Ray,

I hope this email doesn't find you dead inside, because that's exactly where your reply is going to find me and Rich. If this "holding tank" was meant to strip away our will to live, congrats—mission accomplished. We shed our last sliver of sanity this morning.

I've now spent more hours debating snack replenishment strategy with the KGB, err accounting team than doing anything remotely resembling consulting. If you're privy to some secret plan for a new Cold War where I'm stuck on the Soviet side, please share—I'd love to know that these "skills" will have value someday. Rich, meanwhile, has memorized OfficeMax's entire

*product catalog, and I'm one minor intern complaint away from discovering
whether IKEA chairs are effective nooses.*

*If there's even a hint of a project that involves anything beyond filling water
jugs or wrangling rodents while being yelled at by junior accountants who've
never been laid, we're on it. Consider this our official white flag—either get
us out of here or notify HR to come collect what's left.*

Cheers,
Brandon

Just kidding. In reality, Rich and I had cut back on the evening cocktails as
our spirits dimmed with each passing week. That morning, we channeled our
frustration into a brutal leg day workout. I'm not going to say leg day saved my
career. But there's no doubt that the stress relief that exercise offered provided
just enough fuel to ask for help in a way that actually warranted a positive
response—rather than driving it away, like Mr. Banks did in the Admirals Club.

The real email was short and simple:

Subject: Project and staffing touch base

*Hi Ray, we're struggling a good bit. Do you mind coming on-site? Attached
please find the recent request we received along with a few others we found
just a bit demoralizing.*

Brandon

Ray showed up the next day. He was our concierge at the Admirals Club. He
experienced firsthand shock when he saw our dystopian Terminal C. He toured
the workspace, read more of our request logs, and admired our art installations
made from snacks and office supplies. He held up one of our "waste disposal"
flyers with a puzzled look before setting it down to speak with us.

"It could use more detail. We get it. We're still not sure which bins to utilize to
discard our MBAs and Brandon's law degree yet," Rich said to break the ice.

"You can still make jokes. That's a good sign. I'm... wow, I'm speechless, but also,
sorry. Really. I had no idea. Look, you're both rockstars. I... I'll get you out of
here stat. This just isn't okay. This is how you lose people."

"When you say 'lose' people?" I asked.

"Quit. C'mon," Ray retorted.

"We just wanted to make sure," Rich added, and we all laughed.

"Alright, I get it. Okay, take next week off. You're never coming back here. I've got some ideas. We'll find something else. We just may have to separate you two."

"We'll survive," we said in unison. "Jinx."

"Wow. This really was that bad," Ray said, as we both nodded.

"Are you going to, ya know, nix this project?" Rich asked, making the guillotine motion. "I just can't imagine this being the 'right fit' for anyone you didn't wish terminal illness upon."

Ray chuckled, "Absolutely not. They're paying rack rates. We'll use it as a halfway house for folks on performance improvement plans."

"Brutal. But if you need suggestions on replacements, we've got some great ideas," I offered.

"Okay, don't push it," Ray jokingly interjected. "I'm assuming sushi fits with your crazy diets?"

I managed to avoid a Banks-like meltdown at the Admirals Club. With enough fuel in the tank, Rich and I had a candid and productive conversation with Ray about the project. Because of our approach, Ray was eager to help us—he wanted to get us on the plane, not leave us stranded at C26. Surviving a tough project was only part of being properly fueled; I also needed it to keep the bigger picture in focus—to remember why I was gaining this experience in the first place.

Rich and I never worked on a deal together again. Save the Kleenex; we still catch up monthly.

The Bin's Just Not Going to Shut

I had a goal: to run the M&A show one day, to be that person on the call with Wayne. I probably should've written it on a notecard and tossed it in my dopp kit as a daily reminder. I remained focused on learning the skills needed to get there, but I struggled with knowing when to move on. Deep down, I wasn't interested in climbing the partner ladder. But knowing where I wanted to go wasn't enough—I needed fuel to keep that vision in focus. Otherwise, I risked shoving my career track, my bag, in an overhead bin where it wouldn't fit.

Without the right fuel, you risk losing sight of what matters. In a world full of type-A personalities, it's easy to convince yourself that you need to keep your focus fixated upwards, on promotions. If you keep climbing when it's not meant for you, you end up like the Banks' bags—shuffled to the back or tossed under the plane, only to reach your destination much later than planned.

Thanks to Ray, future projects with the firm heightened my roles and sharpened those skills that I needed. But as it goes in the world of professional services: if you want that bump, you must jump. No, not that kind of bump, my i-banking friends. A title bump, and so I leaped firms. Time for a rodeo with PwC.

It wasn't a bad decision. And let's be honest, loyalty in professional services is rarer than honesty in a George Santos congressional campaign. After a quick first project, word got out that I had a law degree. How I'd used it was of little importance; its mere existence boosted our quals to bid on a series of high-profile deals. Yes, sometimes that's how it works. We won the pitch, and away I went.

The client wanted to sell multiple business units. I partnered with a brilliant, three-headed exec team: Lisa, Katherine, and Nicole. To this day, they remain some of the sharpest folks I've ever worked with. The work itself? Stimulating. We lived at the five-point intersection of strategic planning, deal structuring, negotiations, execution, and operational transitions. We touched six continents daily. I loved it. This was exactly what I'd heard on that seminal phone call with Wayne. But now, I was no longer in learning mode. I navigated and resolved the client's gatequakes. This was it. It was my show.

We closed three transactions. I started to wonder: do I really need to leave consulting? I was leading deals here, but as a revenue generator rather than a cost center. Job security, and there were years' worth of transactions left to lead for this prolific client. Partner track, maybe? I mean, surely we can close the bin over the bag, right?

Then I got yanked from the client.

After the third deal closed, a brief lull gave my managing partner an opening. He saw a chance to leverage my friendship with an M&A VP to win work at a new client. It worked. The new gig started part-time but quickly evolved to full-time. Meanwhile, my former client's work picked up steam. I found myself double-staffed, juggling two projects across global time zones. I knew I had to choose one project. The new project involved IT roadmapping; the former, leading deals. No contest—I fit best in the former. Shockingly, the managing partner disagreed. Bin closure failure incoming.

"Sorry about the double duty. That was my mistake. But here's the deal: you could return to the old client and run the same deal processes. Great reps if you wanted to run corporate development, sure, but it won't set you up for managing director or partner track," the managing partner said in his office.

"Even with years of work ahead and millions in revenue for the firm?" I asked.

"Yes. Look, it's a dying company. Finite revenue. And you don't make MD or partner as a deep subject matter expert. We need people who can sell and lead any project, build and staff a team. I need you miles wide and a foot deep. Right now, you're a foot wide and miles deep. This new project helps with that," he explained.

Now you see why I needed that note in my dopp kit. The managing partner spelled it out for me: the project was perfect preparation for leading corporate development—the M&A function—at a company. That's what I wanted. So why was I still forcing myself down the partner track? It was like trying to make "fetch" happen; it wasn't, just like an overstuffed overhead bin won't close. If I kept at it, I'd end up delaying my real goal, potentially arriving dead last like the Banks.

Why was I stuck? Ego. And maybe, just maybe, I was running low on an important fuel source. The gym game was strong, but mentally, I was starting to drift. Then one Sunday morning, Karla's sermon on "calling" hit me hard. Making partner clearly wasn't my calling. It sparked conversations with friends and fellow congregants—some of whom were SMU alums—that opened my mind, and eventually, some important doors.

I'm not suggesting that my desire to run deals was some kind of spiritual calling. It wasn't that deep. But Karla's sermon helped me see that I needed to give up control and let go of my pride. Maybe I'd never get the chance to lead M&A for a company—but I'd never find out if I kept trying to force myself into a consulting career that clearly wasn't the right fit. It took some time to accept this reality—not as long as trying to find your ride at LAX arrivals, but long enough. Eventually, I took my bag out of the overhead when I knew the bin wasn't going to close.

As a travel snob, it was embarrassing to admit that my bag wasn't going to fit and to check it instead. But breezing by baggage claim wouldn't be as humiliating as fighting my way to the back of the plane to get it later. At least on the conveyor it would be marked with a "priority" tag. I went back to the original client's project—a clear sign of where I wanted to take my career. The promotion didn't come, and it still stung amidst the celebrations of those who climbed another rung, but I knew I had made the right choice.

Avoid the Salmon

The Banks' late arrival home happened largely because they had to fight their way backward for their bags—going "upstream" against the current of passengers.

I'd made my decision, but I hadn't given my notice yet. Something kept gnawing at me—like I still had this irrational urge to put my bag back overhead, twist it, turn it and keep trying. If I left, would people still send me the memes? Would I still be part of the inside jokes? And most importantly, would I lose all of my airline and hotel status?

"Brandon, I think you know exactly what you need to do," Fred said before a FlyWheel class. Fred was more than an instructor—he was a pilot along my journey, and a Bain alum. He understood my conundrum.

"Yeah, I know," I replied, glancing around at the familiar faces—the family of friends that had become my "Riches" at the spin studio. "Alright, I'm not making this decision until after class. What's that *Friday Night Lights* quote again? Clear eyes, full h–"

"I. Don't want. Your life," Maria jokingly interrupted with a faux twang. She was my trusty bike neighbor and also shared my love of champagne and tequila. "Just kidding!" she said.

"Ha, that's *Varsity Blues*, but probably more on-point," I said, laughing before we began class.

After the sweat session, I threw my towel in the laundry bin. Fred gave me that look; he wasn't going to let me leave without knowing my choice. He raised his left eyebrow and tilted his head.

"Don't worry! I'm giving my notice!" I said, throwing my hands up as though I was surrendering. "But, why is this so damn hard?"

"Up or out, man. That's why. It's funny, Brandon. It convinces you that 'out' is the worst place you can be, so you equate it to 'down and out' and falling behind. It makes you feel like a quitter or you're settling."

Fred always had a knack for deep truths after class. We also shared similar fuel sources, so I took his words of wisdom heartily.

Where did my focus really need to be? Out and maybe even downward, but not in a negative way. It wasn't a demotion. I needed to look for navigational beacons and runway lights. I wasn't going to find them if I only stared up. That holding pattern I'd mentioned at the outset? I was in one here.

The following day, I failed to give my notice to the firm. Sadly, it took another three weeks. But I did it eventually. I'd soon direct corporate development and strategy efforts at a building products company that recently went public. It was a big step towards leading the M&A show myself. Lisa, Katherine, and Nicole were thrilled for me. The firm's partners actually were, too. I even got one of those awkward send-off parties where colleagues whispered "Take me with you" in your ear after a few drinks.

I dodged a Shane-level fiasco—no backtracking, no swimming upstream. Fuel kept me airborne until I saw the runway lights. It kept my attitude strong through the bad projects, so people wanted to help me, recognizing my resilience and readiness for new opportunities. And the skills I picked up readied me for the new job. Fuel also re-centered my focus so I didn't try to force my bag and end up where I needed to be dead last. It let me move on.

Maybe it's not the gym or the church pew, but it's still crucial that we find healthy ways to relieve stress and remind ourselves that we're not in control and to let go of our pride. The Tetris flunkee helps us understand how to navigate these difficult situations and stay focused thanks to proper fueling. But sometimes it's not just the circumstances at work. Instead, it's the people and personalities that challenge us the most. That's where the conference call deci-bully comes in—to show us how to handle tough personalities without becoming one ourselves. It's time to steer our eyes from the overhead bin and our ears toward the front of the cabin. Just make sure to bring those noise canceling headphones.

Oh yeah, I guess you also now know why protein powder, peanut butter, and bananas still comprise sixty percent of my diet. Never skip leg day. #Gainz

Habit 4: The Conference Call Deci-bully

Conference Call Deci-bully (*noun*): A species of unwavering determination that conducts conference calls at the highest decibel levels possible during the boarding process and disregards their fellow passengers' auditory well-being and livelihood. These creatures partake in a range of activities including:

- Boeing Boardroom Meetings: Unabashedly engages in conference calls that resonate throughout the cabin. Oblivious to the annoyance they generate, they project conversations with a fervor that rivals Howard Dean's 2004 speech after the Iowa caucuses.
- Meteorological Undermining: Believes that the weather conditions outside the plane are inconsequential. Dismisses raindrops as mere illusions and snowflakes as figments of the imagination. Adamantly refuses to accept any disruptions caused by the elements, persisting in requests of the crew for immediate departure and arrival times regardless of meteorological reality.
- Nonchalant Nodding: Responds with dismissive nods when confronted by flight attendants to conclude conversations and stow away laptops. Believes the simple act of acknowledging the request absolves them of any social obligation. Continues their vocal marathon after confrontation but in a still-conspicuous "whisper." Hides the laptop anywhere but the location mandated by the FAA.

The Fix: You Want to... But Probably Shouldn't

Gasp dramatically at the end of each sentence. Pass notes, pretending to contribute insightful comments as part of the ongoing conversation. Include an "invoice" for your time billed for the unexpected participation in the conference call.

As Heard Throughout the Cabin

There is no activity I enjoy more than snow skiing. Bar none. If I had to choose between the mountains and the beach for the rest of my life, I'd choose the mountains without hesitation. My dad first put me on skis at age three, and I've upheld the family tradition for thirty-nine years and counting. Each ski season, I aim for three to five trips, some with friends and at least one with my family. Seeing my eighty-year-old father still hitting the slopes fills me with one simple thought: goals. It sets the bar high for my own future.

While I'm open to various ski trip destinations, "partiality" doesn't even begin to describe my affinity for one particular mountain—Beaver Creek, Colorado. I love the terrain and know the mountain like the back of my hand. The staff maintains it impeccably, and the terrain skis big even if there's less acreage than nearby Vail or Breckenridge. My favorite part? Rarely any lift lines. On second thought, maybe I should shut up. It sucks; it's horrible. Stay far, far away.

A major advantage of skiing at Beaver Creek is its proximity to the Eagle-Vail (EGE) airport. Within just thirty minutes of landing, visitors can find themselves in Beaver Creek village, provided they or their driver take full advantage of the autobahn-like speed limits on I-70. At EGE, airlines fly mainline aircraft, a.k.a. non-regional jets, and divert much less often here than they do at Aspen or Telluride. Although takeoffs and landings here can still feel like riding a go-kart sans brakes on a bumpy cobblestone road at a sixty-degree angle, the time saved on the ground makes up for it—and a few in-flight cocktails can ease the trepidations of anxious passengers. The semi-recent terminal rebuild at EGE offers picturesque views of the Sawatch range and Elk Mountains, comfortable seating, and even a welcoming bar, making it a truly convenient and pleasant experience. Okay, I'll stop sounding like a paid advertisement.

Perhaps the biggest benefit of flying into EGE is the avoidance of Denver International Airport. I get it, most people want to reach ten-thousand steps between deplaning and retrieving their luggage. Also, prairie dogs are cute. Who doesn't enjoy spotting the little creatures popping their heads in and out of the ground in the medians on the thirty-minute journey from the terminal to the rental car facility? Or maybe it's thirty minutes once you get past the demonic horse statue, rightfully nicknamed "Bluecifer," with his illuminated red eyes – yet no visible power supply. By the time you get to a rental car and start the two-hour journey towards the mountains, a flight into EGE would already have you mountainside with an Aperol Spritz in hand.

EGE is an easy airport, but the passengers who traverse its concourse? Not always as smooth as the corduroy runs at Beaver Creek.

In late March one year, I arrived at EGE with plenty of time to spare. A late spring storm cell was headed our way, but the radar indicated that the snowfall wouldn't arrive for a couple of hours. As I hopped out of the SUV and began helping the driver unload my ski bag from the roof rack, the inbound flight roared as it touched down half a football field away.

"Well, that's a great sound – assuming you wanted to leave. You should be free and clear to skedaddle before the weather arrives," the driver said.

"Too bad," I thought. This is the only location where I'd welcome a flight cancellation if it meant another day on the slopes.

As I made my way inside toward the check-in area, I couldn't help but notice a family of three gathered in the airline's priority check-in line. And when I say "gathered," I mean the wife and husband were accosting the check-in agent while their son nestled his wheelchair and leg cast against a luggage cart to support the last of the family's mountain of bags. Evidently, they sought to check in the entire Rocky Mountains for their flight back to Atlanta. The father, dressed for Hilton Head in a blue Masters polo and salmon chinos, was leaning over the counter, trying to peek at the desk agent's screen. He appeared quite unhappy as the agent smiled but wouldn't budge. She looked like a young "fun" grandma from Texas and used her red nails to push some of the blonde curls out of her face to pass the time. I sensed this process might take a while, but I still got in the queue.

Fifteen minutes went by without resolution. Thinking I could avoid a delayed check-in process and more quickly get to a pre-flight cocktail, I ducked under the stanchion to my right to join the standard bag drop line, which seemed to move at a much quicker pace. Suddenly, two families of five with two to three bags each beat me to the punch. Ugh.

As I ducked again to move myself, my carry-on, and my ski bag back to the priority line, my left earbud died. I will never understand why the left and right earbuds do not maintain identical charging life, but I'll save that rant for another day. I placed them both back in the charger and into my bag when I was graced with the terse voice of the father with the bubbly but resolute agent. His name was Mr. Whitaker, Forest Pennington Whitaker IV. Of course he had a numerical suffix. He was slightly overweight and apparently enjoyed feasting on inconveniencing others.

Mr. Whitaker was attempting to take a conference call while simultaneously explaining to the ticketing agent that, due to his purchase of first-class seats, the airline was obligated to accept their plethora of bags on board.

"Of course, sir, I understand. We value all our passengers, and your bags are certainly welcome. I wish I weighed as little as this one. However, I'm afraid we still need this plane to take off, and even first-class bags have to abide by the laws of physics." The ticketing agent smiled before Mr. Whitaker jumped in.

"Ma'am. Listen. Cut the crap. I've traveled before. Many times. I only fly first, and I do that so I don't end up in situations where people like you think you can drag me along on one of your power trips. This is getting ridiculous. I'm not afraid to call the airline," the father interrupted, "Hey – hold on one second," he barked into his earbuds, better charged than mine apparently. "The airline is trying to bar us from bringing our stuff back. These flights were two grand a piece. How much do you have to pay for good service these days?"

He turned back to those of us waiting. "Unreal, right? Good luck dealing with these clowns," he said, loud enough for us to hear him over our own headphones.

The ticketing agent maintained an unflappable demeanor, blending the poise of Meryl Streep's *Iron Lady* with Doralee Rhodes' wit and charm. She skillfully handled Mr. Whitaker's condescending remarks without even offering an eye roll.

"Are they moving the whole mountain?" asked the father behind me, his family with a reasonable amount of luggage in tow and all injury-free. I laughed and nodded back to him, when Mrs. Whitaker decided to intervene.

With her long blond hair, cat-eye glasses, and clunky turquoise jewelry, Mrs. Whitaker was an Aldi-brand Jennifer Coolidge. She looked as if she'd just auditioned for a *Real Housewives* show, and I suspected her breakfasts often included white wine. She turned, eyeing the growing line of passengers, and decided to join forces with her husband against the agent. "Can you just... get your manager out here so we can rectify this? You're holding up the line for other priority passengers." I suspected her name was Karen.

She turned back to us, pointed at the agent, and threw her hands up, mouthing, "She's awful." At least, I think that's what she tried to say—her limited facial movement and fresh collagen injections made it hard to read her lips.

The agent saw the growing line and made a swift judgment call.

"Well, alrighty now! Let's just start bringing those bags of yours right over here so the other passengers can check in for the flight," the ticketing agent stated as she hauled the remaining bags off the cart and began to tag them. Forest

Whitaker's volume on his call increased with each of his turns towards those of us waiting in line. As the agent tagged each piece of luggage, he occasionally made gestures implying, "Not sure what the agent's problem is," as if trying to convince us it wasn't his family's luggage causing the fiasco.

Finally, I approached the counter to drop off my skis. "Just one bag, I promise. It was only forty-four pounds when I came here and there's less in it now."

The ticketing agent laughed in relief. "Thank you! You're all set, sir. Have a great flight."

As I walked away toward security, I heard her instruct a man placing bags on the carousel, "Hold your horses with those. We need to make sure we label the previous parties' bags with 'heavy' tags before they go on the conveyor belt." Yeah, this saga was far from over.

I made my way through TSA and found some real estate at the bar. The airport was bustling, but I swore I still heard Mr. Whitaker on his conference call. I received a notification that it was time to board, closed out my tab and made my way to the gate.

As the boarding process commenced, Mrs. Whitaker emphatically informed the gate agent that their family needed to pre-board first due to their injured son. The gate agent politely acquiesced, but Mrs. Whitaker insisted on standing at the scanner disallowing any others to beat them to their seats. Meanwhile, Mr. Whitaker's voice grew louder as he continued his call in front of the entire gate house.

I boarded the plane shortly after the Whitakers. Forest's voice bellowed as he stood in the aisle messing with his backpack overhead, blocking my path to the emergency exit row.

He finally placed both in the bins overhead. "Yeah, I'm still here," he barked into his headphones.

I sauntered over to my seat in the "poor man's" first class—the emergency exit row. Just as I settled in, a flight attendant flagged me down to inform me of my new seat in row two. Real first class! Score, and yes, consider this a humble brag. A complimentary upgrade to or from EGE is noteworthy. I didn't frame my boarding pass, but the thought crossed my mind.

I grabbed my bags and made the awkward salmon swim upstream to row two. It's the airline status "walk of shame"—everyone knew I wasn't a paying first-class passenger. I thought I heard several passengers utter "freeloader" under their breaths. A flight attendant helped me play Tetris with the overhead bags to make room for mine. That's when Mr. Whitaker turned around and stood up.

"Hold on a sec, George," he said into his headphones before turning his attention to us. "Yeah, let's not move our bags. We've got some fragile things in there. That's why we boarded first to make sure they were secure," he barked. "Yeah, still here. You wouldn't believe this flight."

"Real gem, that family. Not sure it's an upgrade up here today given the racket," my seat neighbor said as I took my seat. "If you need more space, I can put one of my bags under the seat in front of me."

"I'm all set, but thank you," I said. The Whitaker's son sat across the aisle from me. Just in front of him were his parents. Forest's right leg crossed over his left nearly into the aisle, showcasing a leather driving shoe worn without socks. Then he began to kick the back of his foot out of the shoe. He placed his barefoot on the bulkhead wall in front of him. He now offended two senses.

Sidebar: I lived in the South for years and never understood the appeal of wearing leather shoes without socks. It's beyond foul and deserving of fines, maybe even imprisonment. End rant.

As Mr. Whitaker continued to drone on about the lease negotiations, passengers cringed and groaned substantially above their breaths. The kiddo, fully immersed in video games without headphones and the volume turned up, showcased a hereditary trait of noise discourtesy. Mrs. Whitaker naturally ordered a pre-flight Chardonnay. The crew exchanged amused glances with several passengers who marveled at the family's spectacle. The boarding process seemed to crawl along as Mr. Whitaker's voice reverberated throughout the plane. I was half tempted to offer him some suggestions that might get the negotiations sealed so the cabin could enjoy some peace and quiet.

Mr. Whitaker turned up his volume another decibel as he declared the final terms to include in the contract. Patience thinned throughout the cabin. Even Mrs. Whitaker shushed her husband. As the tension on the Airbus reached its peak, a voice boomed over the PA system. The announcement caught everyone's attention, temporarily drowning out Mr. Whitaker's incessant chatter. The pilot's voice filled the cabin, explaining the situation with a mix of professionalism and forced cheerfulness. Due to weight restrictions given the altitude and runway length, the crew would need to reorganize and prioritize the cargo hold. It was a painstaking task that would require a bit of time that we did not have if we wanted to make it out before the storm. On cue, the skies outside began to whiten, signaling the pending arrival of snow showers. A delay grew more inevitable with each passing minute, likely thanks to the Whitaker family and their mountain of luggage.

Suddenly, the crew shut the boarding door, providing a glimmer of hope that they might sort out the weight restriction issue and get us airborne.

A flight attendant instructed Mr. Whitaker to finish his call. He dismissively nodded and held up three fingers, signaling he needed just three more minutes. The flight attendant insisted he hang up immediately. Her expression barely held together—a mix of strained politeness and the desperate look of someone who just wanted to hit the hang-up button, or this particular passenger, herself. Mr. Whitaker grunted but finally concluded his call. Relief filled the cabin, and many passengers exchanged knowing glances and stifled laughter, resisting the urge to applaud. Why? Because clapping on airplanes is never a good look.

Mr. Whitaker leaned forward toward the seated flight attendant, "What's the hold up? Why haven't we backed up from the gate?" he demanded to know.

"Sir, as we explained, we have a weight-restricted flight—and given the storm, we are trying to ensure we load the plane correctly for everyone's safety."

"Seriously? C'mon now," he replied, apparently with no remembrance of his encounter with the desk agent. He then demanded to know precisely when the flight would depart and arrive, as if the flight attendants and crew possessed divine powers to control the weather. "I've taken off in the Caymans with far scarier skies than this. We packed similarly. You've got to be kidding me. Do I at least have time to take a leak?"

"Sir, we would advi—" the flight attendant said before the pilot came back on over the PA.

"Good news. We have finished loading the flight to proper weight capacity. Some bags have been deplaned but will arrive at your final destination, just a bit later. You can check the app, and you will receive further notification from our team if they're not arriving with our flight. We have a ten-minute window to get out of here based on decreasing visibility so we are going to taxi and get this bird in the air. Flight attendants – prepare the cabin for departure."

Mrs. Whitaker's voice pierced through the cabin as she pointed, her hand trembling: "Forest, Forest! There go our bags!" The flight was already rolling. I tried not to laugh, but seriously—stop the plane? I've heard some wild requests, but that one really took the cake. I imagined the check-in agent's smile as the bags returned to her desk inside the terminal. She had every reason to be proud—not only for keeping her cool and maintaining professionalism in the face of the Whitakers' antics, but also for managing to let them face some natural consequences of their behavior. Maybe, just maybe, this experience would nudge them to reconsider their ways before their next flight.

As Applied in Reality

Self-Priority Passengers

On this journey, we've faced setbacks that forced us to shift from tunnel vision, acknowledge our limitations, and power through environments that made us question our life choices—and maybe reach for a drink before noon. Along the way, we've spotted pilots, gate agents, and even concierges who were there to help... if we bothered to ask.

But then there are the people who refuse to help—the ones who only look out for themselves, hogging all the cargo space and glory like it's their birthright. We've all dealt with a Whitaker: the human roadblock, someone so self-absorbed that they request bends to the rules of gravity. Whether it's someone on a flight or in a meeting, they're out there, causing problems just so they get what they want. The temptation to escalate is real. Unfortunately, physical assault, while tempting, is frowned upon—and fully prosecutable in all fifty states.

The Whitakers of the world are annoying, sure, but their behavior isn't illegal. Sometimes it's even rewarded. And if you're like me, you run into them often— not just in airports. So, we need other ways to deal with them, that don't result in fines or imprisonment.

But there's a kicker: while it's easy to laugh as the Whitakers' bags get left behind, we're all one bad day away from becoming one. Our own egos sneak in, and before we know it, we're the person we can't stand in the check-in line. So, the goal here is twofold. First, learn to deal with Whitakers. Second, make sure you're not becoming one yourself. Otherwise, you might arrive without your bags.

Fortunately, the check-in agent at EGE gave us a sneak peek at the playbook, showing how to handle Whitakers with wit, grit, and a touch of humility.

A Counter with Wit, Humility, and Grit

Let's tackle handling the Whitakers first.

The agent handled the Whitakers thanks to plenty of experience with difficult passengers. I imagine the slight fear of what customers could do— even when they were wrong—kept her from giving them the treatment they probably deserved. After all, the risk of getting fired loomed large when "the customer is always right." But she didn't roll over. She stood firm, kept her cool, and let the "heavy tags" speak for themselves. Sly and smart, she let things unfold.

She had a bit of Maggie Thatcher in her, but there was also a strong dose of Dolly Parton's Doralee Rhodes from *9 to 5*. Dolly knew how to handle tough situations with grit and wit, both on-screen and off. And just like the agent, Dolly had her run-ins with the Whitakers of the world.

In a notorious 1977 interview, Barbara Walters asked Dolly, "Where I come from, would I have called you a hillbilly?"—barely masking the condescension. It wasn't an isolated moment; Dolly's looks, intelligence, and upbringing were questioned regularly. Yet she always responded with a smile and razor-sharp humor.

"I'm not offended by all the dumb blonde jokes because I know I'm not dumb... and I also know I'm not blonde," she quipped.

Like the check-in agent, Dolly knew she had to work with the press—even when they were patronizing—if she wanted to succeed. She let her work and wit speak for themselves. Humor? Check. Self-deprecation? All day. And when none of that worked, she gritted her teeth and kept moving forward. Wit, humility, and grit were Dolly's "heavy tags"—she let her talent do the lifting, knowing that sometimes the best move is letting things fall into place.

I'd say it worked. Dolly is a national treasure and icon, and anyone who doubled down on doubting her? Well, let's just say their bags didn't make it on the plane.

Yeah, don't expect my story to have quite the same meteoric rise.

First-Class Tickets

Most people can easily name a Whitaker or two from their work history—maybe even fill more pages than this book if you've been around long enough. And if you can't think of one, well, you might want to skip ahead a few sections in this chapter that discuss self-reflection.

The Whitakers of the workplace often arrive with credentials from "target schools," those institutions ranked by *US News & World Report* as producing the best and brightest. Firms flock here for recruiting purposes as glossy resumes look shiny in quals and pitch decks and help justify fees. After all, who but Ivy League MBAs from McKinsey could figure out—at a cool four million dollars—that trash cans might help reduce New York City's rat problem?

Sigh. Rich and I would've done it for just half of that.

Clearly, it's not everyone from these schools or firms. The vast majority aren't Whitakers. But for those who are, their behavior doesn't end at the airport. Instead of flashing a first-class boarding pass, they awkwardly lead conversations with their alma mater. Instead of insisting on cargo space for entrapped grizzlies in a Rimowa luggage collection, they're demanding better compensation, top projects, and expedited promotions—all because of that one piece of paper.

In the wild, you'll usually find them lurking where there's overlap between one firm's bottom-tier target schools and another's top picks. It's a never-ending hierarchy—the schools that are lower on the list for a top firm are the crown jewels for the next one down, and so on. When someone with a higher-ranked diploma feels stuck at a firm deemed low on their prospect list, watch out—they'll be bringing along a loaded luggage cart of resentment.

I didn't have to worry about this scenario. My graduate schools at the time weren't on any consulting firm target lists. SMU was, sure, but by the time I was working, that was old news. I was just lucky to be in the room. Imagine how unlucky the Whitakers felt to call me their senior, their colleague, or direct report when they showed up to work.

I enjoyed working with most of my colleagues—this isn't an exposé. In fact, healthy banter turned many of us from coworkers into lifelong friends. And don't tell the firms I leaked this, but there were more people like me than you'd expect. The firms rewarded hard work if you could deliver, regardless of pedigree, which drove the Whitaker types only further insane.

I took the cheap shots in stride. Compensation discrepancies were as confidential as the Wi-Fi password at the Centurion Lounge. Whitakers, however, made sure you knew exactly what they earned—while pretending they thought everyone made the same. A few even asked me to omit my educational background from my bios in pitch decks. One or two even went as far as saying they wouldn't have signed off on my transfer or hire. I respected the honesty, though—it gave me a clear face to picture on the bag during boxing class.

But, like the check-in agent at EGE, snapping wasn't an option. Keeping my job meant playing the long game and sharpening my M&A skills. I had to work alongside these folks—whether I liked it or not—if I had any hope of moving up (and eventually, out). Wit, humility, and grit became my go-to tools to get through it.

I learned to laugh at myself long before consulting—pairing wit and humility was easy. With that, most jokes turned from condescension to banter. I'd hear, "So, what's the graduation requirement in South Carolina and Mississippi? Passing a sobriety test and making sure you know your sister from your cousin?" I'd fire back, "Actually, I just had to color inside the lines and walk a straight line while saying my ABCs—more than someone could handle after their third martini last night." It broke the ice.

I also took on tasks my colleagues hated—the kinds of things an Ivy grad never imagined they'd be doing after graduation. "I thought I'd be changing the world, building things," they'd say. "You do build things. Decks and models, because that's what this job is all about." Meanwhile, I wasn't brownnosing. If I wanted to run M&A, not just advise on it, I needed to understand the nitty-gritty.

Over time, my grit—and my work—started to speak for itself. When clients requested teams for future projects, I was honored to be called out by name. I wanted to make the firm look good, even if my team included the occasional asshole. Leadership valued that and rewarded it. And while I didn't always want to work with the Whitakers or pretend their jokes were funny, I found a way to make it work... for the length of the engagement.

But just like the check-in agent at EGE, I learned when to tag the bags as "heavy" and move on. You can only carry so much weight before you risk delaying your own takeoff.

Tag the Bags "Heavy"

I mentioned in the last chapter that I waffled back and forth about leaving consulting. Yes, Fred at FlyWheel was absolutely right about the "up or out" reality being tough, but there was more to it. When people found out what I did, I earned instant credibility—just add a title and stir. They'd look at me like I was smart, important, even accomplished, without a single second of real conversation. M&A strategy consulting was a badge I'd gotten used to wearing, and frankly, that automatic respect was hard to walk away from. It felt like I'd earned my spot in the ranks of a prestigious and impressive crowd. I was going to walk away from that?

The decision became a lot easier the day a certain person marched right up to my desk to check in.

Enter Chad, Forest Whitaker's consulting avatar. Chad made a great first impression, but his shtick wore thin fast. He couldn't stop talking, and he liked himself more than a Kardashian. He never missed a chance to name-drop his MBA program and looked down on anyone whose alma mater didn't pass his sniff test. The irony? His work product was so questionable, people wondered if someone else had taken the GMAT for him.

Chad also loved to brag about turning down an offer from Bain. Nobody believed him, of course, but that didn't stop him from liking every Bain post on LinkedIn. Awkward. We were also pretty sure we'd identified his burner account on Fishbowl.

Even worse, Chad loved to spread misinformation. He claimed he had a better vest collection than me, and even lied about his airline status. After his fifth gin and tonic at the MIA Flagship Lounge, he confessed to using years-old luggage tags to fake United 1K. He was Platinum. Fraud.

While I pondered my career move, Chad pinged me to help with a proposal for Judy, a partner who adored him (and was equally insufferable). His follow-up message? "Just FYI, we're up against BCG on this one. Big dogs. We need to look top-tier, so we're only including Judy, Steve, and me in the official proposal. But will you still look through the materials given your expertise in this arena?"

"Dear God, please don't let us win," I prayed.

It was laughable—only Chad and Judy would ask something so audacious. Still, I gave it my best, offering up content suggestions in the deck, tagging the bags heavy where it mattered, and pointing out where their current approach didn't align with the client's RFP. Like at all.

Days later, it became clear Chad and Judy had ignored my comments on a prep call. They were prepping for tactical execution like we'd already won the deal, with no adjustments to the proposal. When I raised concerns, Judy scolded me for questioning her judgment and expertise. Chad pinged me in parallel, "Not cool dude." By that point, I wasn't even worried anymore—I knew we didn't stand a chance. The materials addressed none of the client's key questions. "Sorry bro."

On pitch day, Chad and Judy pulled the team aside: "No one speaks unless we give you permission." I had a feeling where this was headed.

Three minutes into the presentation, the client's executive team started exchanging confused glances. At the five-and-a-half-minute mark, one of them interrupted, "I'm going to stop you right there. I think there's been a mistake. What you're discussing right now doesn't really address what we expressed in the RFP. Did you confuse ours with someone else's request by chance?"

Ouch.

I could feel Judy and Chad staring at me, waiting for me to chime in. The subject matter was my arena. Had they asked, I might have helped, but I was just following their rules. Chad pulled up the RFP on the screen, and sure enough—they'd simply fucked up. Big time. Then the fun began.

Judy and Chad fumbled the recovery epically. It was like listening to a verbal circular reference warning. Think Sarah Palin discussing her favorite newspapers with Katie Couric or Nancy Pelosi's "Good Morning, Sunday morning" reboot mid-interview with George Stephanopoulos. The client even tried to help, but Chad and Judy just kept talking. I could almost hear the luggage conveyor whirring behind us, their bags tagged heavy and on their way back to the drawing board. Internally, I smiled, as I imagined the gate agent did as she watched the Whitakers' bags return.

The company, unsurprisingly, chose BCG.

For me, it was a turning point. I'd learned to handle the Whitakers and even tag their bags heavy when needed. It was great practice because Whitakers are everywhere on our journey, But the more I navigated these situations in consulting, the more I realized my bags were ready to leave, too. I didn't need to fight for a seat at the Whitakers' table anymore—I was ready to build my own.

Avoiding Whitaker Syndrome

Handling Whitakers? Check. So what's next—learning how not to be an asshole? Easier said than done. But Dolly gave us the blueprint. The same grit, humility, and wit she used on her critics, she turned on herself. My boss followed the same playbook, so I was lucky enough to learn from the best.

I closed the last chapter with a brief mention that I took a job directing M&A and strategy efforts and left consulting. The opportunity was at a holding company with two operating businesses—one installed flooring, cabinets, and countertops for new home builders, and the other imported and distributed stone slabs. Think marble, granite, quartz—surfaces HGTV would fawn over. My job? To source, negotiate, and close deals with folks who had built their businesses from the ground up and were ready to sell. And yes, I held out hope for some HGTV overlap.

I meant it when I said learned from the best—D'Andre, that's who hired me. He had every right to be a Whitaker but wasn't even close. With an engineering degree from Michigan and an MBA from Wharton, followed by stints on Wall Street and turning around failing enterprises as an interim CEO, CFO, and COO, he could've been insufferable and demanded all the cargo space. But he didn't. He was now the Global Head of Strategy, M&A, and Supply Chain. Essentially, he was the person I'd heard on that call with Wayne—and then some. Now, I'd get to learn from him directly. Well, that is if I didn't screw up the interview.

Our interview took place at a Starbucks in suburban Atlanta. The thirty-minute conversation quickly turned into a two-hour game-planning session. I hadn't even started, much less gotten an offer, but I was already excited. Before we wrapped up, D'Andre had one final housekeeping matter.

"Okay, so," he said, motioning to my suit. "This? Probably not gonna fly in our world."

I'd just come from a client meeting, hence the attire. "Duly noted," I laughed. "Honestly, I was just hoping this interview would be the funeral for my consulting days. Had to dress the part, you know."

"Fair enough," he said with a grin. "Stock up on golf polos. We'll be in touch soon, and maybe schedule a wake for some of that vernacular."

Unlike the sports agency in Orange County, D'Andre actually called back.

D'Andre didn't have to be humble, but he was. I caught glimpses of it during the interview, but soon I'd see how he applied wit, grit, and humility to himself—always playing the long game without ego and getting results.

Take Out the AirPods

If Mr. Whitaker had just taken out his AirPods and heard himself—both his volume and his content—he probably would've changed his tone and tune alike. That's all it took to change my perspective.

On my second day at the new job, we flew to Seattle to scout a potential acquisition. I wore jeans and a polo, and part of me worried my fellow passengers in suits thought I was unemployed. That fear somewhat subsided by week two when we traveled to a Virginia company under letter of intent (LOI), with a few more businesses across the US not too far behind. I wasn't going to lose my airline or hotel status, which was a huge relief.

Then, by week three, a third deal hit. I hopped on a diligence call that included the full spectrum: our team and the seller's advisors, plus the founder himself. The advisors went first, dropping their names, titles, and deal sheets like I'd done so many times in my consulting days. When my turn came, I felt the old instinct to puff up, prove I could go toe-to-toe with them. I kept it under sixty seconds, but I ran through my list.

"Lordy. So, the folks on your side don't speak any English either? I already knew y'all couldn't do normal math with all this EBITD-whatever. Hope y'all enjoy paying off all that student debt," the seller said with a laugh.

Shit.

"Don't worry, Darryl. We're deprogramming him quickly," D'Andre said, shooting me a wink. "Now, let's not get you into any debt racking up fees on this call."

"Whew, that's right. Let's get to it," Darryl responded.

After the call, D'Andre put me on a performance improvement plan. Not really, we actually debriefed with our team of advisors via phone. Darryl's business was highly profitable, but his data was messy—across the board. That mess turned into some jokes by our advisors, poking fun at Darryl's lack of sophistication and education. I'll admit, I quietly agreed with most of what I heard, but I kept my laughter internal as I saw D'Andre shake his head. We outlined next steps and ended the call.

"Didn't mean to call you out earlier," D'Andre said, sliding some papers my way. "The vocabulary will come—just like the attire. The latter took me a minute, too. It's a different world, but don't let those guys on the phone fool you into thinking Darryl's a dummy. If anything, that's us. No offense."

"Ha. None taken," I replied, flipping through the stack of documents he handed over.

Darryl was set to pocket $75 million at closing. He was the sole shareholder. As I thumbed through the valuation, my eyes caught on a list of EBITDA add-backs that included a helicopter and what could only be described as a "redneck" yacht. A few pages later, I saw that Darryl also owned the land where his business was housed—office space, yard, the whole nine yards. We'd be leasing it back from him at $25,000 a month. I must have raised an eyebrow because D'Andre chimed back in.

"Take a look at the excluded assets list," he added, smirking slightly.

Well, okay then. Darryl loved cars. I thought I was doing all right with my BMW SUV—it still had the factory warranty, after all—but apparently not. Darryl collected fully restored classics like his 1967 and 1968 Shelby Mustangs, as well as a pair of Chevrolet Camaro Z28s. Not content with just American muscle, he also had a flair for the European, flaunting a Porsche 911, an Aston Martin DB7, and a Ferrari Testarossa.

"Did we order a background check on this guy?" I asked, only semi-joking.

"When Darryl graduated high school, his parents gave him a choice: college education or a pickup truck. He picked the truck and learned how to install flooring. The guy built this empire from the ground up. All that cash? It's his, and all taxed at long-term cap gains rates. Sure, the deals we'll do here are smaller than what you used to see, but Darryl is the norm. And I don't know about you, but I'd happily take his place over our advisors. They're truly fine folks on the phone. They're smart, no doubt. That's why they're helping us with diligence. But when you really look at those documents, who's really the smart one?"

"This makes me question all my life choices," I said.

"Welcome to the club."

I took out my AirPods and heard myself loud and clear. Judging people when they're winning? That's how you become a Whitaker. D'Andre taught me to apply wit, grit, and humility to myself. Can you laugh at your own shortcomings? Admit you couldn't build what they've built? Can you prove you're pulling your weight to get the deal done for them and not just flashing your résumé? And can you acknowledge the common ground for interests—especially when they can probably afford the nicer things you can't? If you can do that, you'll avoid becoming a Whitaker, earn some respect, make a few friends, and close some deals along the way.

D'Andre and I achieved the company's goal of coast-to-coast operations several months ahead of plan. We consistently outpaced other buyers by building genuine relationships, letting the Whitakers watch their offers deplane like heavy-tagged bags. As D'Andre gave me a longer leash, I earned my reputation as a closer. It all culminated when I sourced two targets that wouldn't just expand our company but open new verticals—including the one that necessitated my flight in the Gate Lice episode. Everything seemed to align.

But winning deals wasn't just about navigating difficult personalities—it was about knowing when to rely on others. Success came easier when I wasn't trying to be the smartest guy in the room.

The real lesson? Knowing when to ask for help, even when your pride says otherwise, and building a network you can count on. That's where the real wins happen. Enter the window seat wobbler, stumbling into our aisle like the town drunk at last call—a not-so-subtle reminder that, sometimes, we all need a hand to steady us on the flight.

Chapter 7

Habit 5: The Window Wobbler

Window Wobbler (*noun*): These are specimens renowned for their remarkable ability to test in parallel the endurance of crew members, fellow passengers, and bodily organs. Key characteristics include:

- Liver Limbo: Demonstrates an unwavering commitment to exploring the physical boundaries of their liver's resilience within the confines of the airline lounge or airport bar pre-departure and in-flight until they are cut off or passed out.
- Verbal Vertigo: Engages in borderline inappropriate commentary directed towards airport employees, crew members, and unsuspecting fellow passengers, reveling in remarks that will conveniently evade their memory come morning.
- Restroom Rendezvous: Assumes the coveted window seat and incessantly disrupt the tranquility of neighboring travelers by frequently rising to attend nature's call, treating the seats in front as notches on a climbing wall.

The Fix: You Want to... But Probably Shouldn't

Anticipate the inevitable as the window wobbler uses the back of your seat as their personal rock-climbing grip. Preemptively hold the seat release button just as they start to pull themselves up, ensuring they get an unexpected free fall back to their seat. As they tumble, act shocked and apologize profusely, claiming you had no idea they were trying to stand up.

As Seen in the Aisleway

At some point, you've probably come across a job listing with a suspiciously wide-ranging list of cities as potential locations. That's code for "you'll be living on airplanes." These aren't random places—they're airline hubs. Airlines hub in cities where they control the most gates and routes, which means frequent travelers can traverse more easily and (theoretically) arrive on time for their meetings.

When you're flying with an airline at their hub, life's a little easier. You'll get customer service options, lounges to duck into for a seat near an outlet, and maybe even drinks and snacks to keep you sane during delays. In some markets, airlines still maintain lounges and support services in an effort to compete with the dominant hub airline. At other airports, some airlines throw in the towel entirely. It's most noticeable at Washington-Dulles.

As a non-United flyer, Dulles is a nightmare. For the outcasts, it operates with the same efficiency as the folks working inside the Capitol building just twenty-six miles down I-66. Non-United flights are few and far between, scheduled in a way that guarantees you'll hit DC rush hour, and the fun doesn't stop there. By the time you've wrestled with the rental car drop-off, survived the rollercoaster ride of the shock-less Hertz shuttle, and made it to the terminal, you've only just begun.

Even as a travel pro, you need a full hour just to navigate from the car drop-off to the gate, weaving around passengers with baggage carts packed like they're moving into a primary residence. Due to the steps and stress, you're Oura ring or Apple watch will certainly detect a workout by the time you arrive at security. If ten percent of the passengers know what they're doing there, consider yourself lucky. On a bustling Thursday afternoon, I was unlucky, thanks in part to the passenger standing right in front of me at the PreCheck line. Meet Kathy.

Kathy insisted to the TSA agent that she had PreCheck, despite it missing from her boarding pass. After a brief back-and-forth, he informed her she'd have to either return to the airline counter or go through regular security. Her argument stretched to a solid four minutes, my patience thinning as my schedule tightened. Thankfully, my phone pinged with a delay notification, so at least I wasn't late—just stuck in her drama.

As Kathy finally swiveled to leave, her overstuffed tote bag caught on her carry-on, and the inevitable happened: the contents spilled across the floor. Passengers immediately bent down to help gather her things, but she snapped, "Don't put your paws on my stuff!" She swatted and shouted at the Good Samaritans as I stepped over her scattered belongings.

You guessed it. That wasn't the last time I'd see her that day.

Once you're through security at Dulles, the adventure's far from over. That's typically when the boarding notification hits, and the clock starts ticking. At least that day, I was spared extra cardio. The signage, while technically correct, was as helpful as a Spider-Man meme, pointing in every direction at once. Families scratched their heads, carts filled with grandparents swerved, and somehow, everyone seemed lost.

The train station area? Straight out of *Blade Runner*. Dim lighting, steel beams, and the hum of the tracks create an industrial ambiance, with illuminated glass casings that felt like what the '80s thought the future would look like. All that was missing was a Vangelis soundtrack—enough time passes waiting for the train that you can hear the opening chords of one their long tracks.

After a two-minute ride and two escalators, I finally reached the concourse. With no lounges or power outlets in the gate houses, it's hard to get any work done in the event of a delay. Lucky for me, I found open real estate in Vino Volo

I sat facing the concourse, drinks with a view. I'd just placed my order and opened my laptop when I saw Kathy again, red-faced and frantic, barreling through the crowd toward the gates. Her tote still had a mind of its own—items spilling out as she weaved through the terminal, shooing away anyone who tried to assist. I returned to my work emails, not expecting another interaction, when suddenly, Kathy dropped into the seat right next to me.

She slapped her boarding pass on the table, and I couldn't help but notice she was on my flight, seated one row behind me. The paper ticket explained two things: her sudden appearance and her blissful ignorance of the delay. With a dramatic flourish, she plopped her iPad down and launched FaceTime, all before the waiter could even reach the table. "Ugh, you won't believe this," she groaned before ordering a flight of white wine.

"So, first off, this airport is, like, a million miles from DC. I swear! Oh, and the airport I put into Google Maps last night was the wrong one. Then, when I finally got here, it took me twenty minutes—twenty minutes!—just to find the ticket counter so I could print my boarding pass. And then, get this, the stupid airline forgot to print TSA PreCheck on my boarding pass. So, when I got to security, they made me go through regular security, which, by the way, was on a completely different level that I couldn't find. Then, I got on the train, absolutely panicked that I'm going to miss my flight. I'm trying to rush past all these oblivious people on the escalators who don't care that I'm in a hurry, only to run to the gate and find out we're delayed more than an hour."

I'd always wondered how rookies managed Dulles. Kathy summed up the pain and suffering in less than a minute. While she was clearly a rookie at the airport, she was no amateur with the wine—polishing off an entire flight in record time. Her scarf and carefully chosen outfit suggested she'd put in effort for her travels, but by now, the unraveling had begun. It was clear that her disheveled state bothered her more than anything else.

"Hey you," she called to the waiter and pointed at her empty glasses. "I'll take another. Just make it an entire flight of the Sonoma Chardonnay this time, please. And maybe a little 'friendlier' on the pours," she added with a nervous smile. I watched her down it as quickly as the first. She must've caught my look of surprise because she blurted, "Flying makes me so uneasy. Oh, that reminds me, I need to take my pills," she said, rummaging through her tote.

The inbound plane finally landed, so I tidied up a few slides, sent the latest investment committee deck to the team, and closed my tab. As I got up to leave, I noticed Kathy order another Chardonnay, sneakily pour it into her rose-gold Stanley, and then ask for the check.

At the gate, I immediately felt sorry for the lone gate agent, caught in the eye of the gate lice storm. Delayed passengers shouted over each other like reporters at a press conference. The scene highlighted just how little the airline invested in its operations at Dulles. I couldn't really blame them, considering they used Reagan National as a hub just down the road. This begged the question—why didn't these folks just make the short commute and catch a direct flight from there? Amateurs.

A few minutes passed when Kathy stumbled up beside me and asked, "Are we boarding yet?"

I shook my head and watched a people mover straight from the set of *Star Wars* drive by outside.

The gate agent scanned her badge and unlocked the door. She opened boarding to those included in the airline's invite-only status, the Skull & Bones society of the skies. Kathy approached the gate. The agent read Kathy's ticket and said she'd need to wait.

Kathy stepped to the side, which proved to be a mistake. When the gate agent called Group 1, the entrance flooded, and Kathy got caught in the hustle, scrambling to push her way back into line.

I took my aisle seat in row three. Five minutes later, Kathy finally showed up, moving slowly to row four, her balance thrown off by the wine. Her aisle seat neighbor asked if she'd switch seats with his wife, who was across the aisle from me.

"No, no, no. I need the window, or I'll have a panic attack," Kathy said without hesitation.

Time to settle the "seat switch" debate. Look, I'm Team Aisle all day, but I get the appeal of the window seat. You can zone out to the view, avoid getting up for anyone, and it's comforting. But the request to trade seats? That's a personal choice. If someone's picked a seat, there's usually a reason. I was Team Kathy on this one. End rant.

I couldn't, however, defend her approach to actually getting into the seat. Kathy yanked on chair backs like a climber scaling Everest without a Sherpa. Mine took the first hit, her grip so forceful I almost hit the seat release button out of spite. But I showed restraint. As she finally settled, she thudded into the seat in front of her repeatedly, leaving my seat neighbor looking like she was cruising over speed bumps. The flight attendant came by to check if anyone wanted a pre-departure drink.

"Oh, thank God. Do you have a wine list?" Kathy asked.

"I do! It's quite long. Red, white, or sparkling?" the flight attendant replied.

Kathy gave a playful wave. "Oh, you're funny. If the white's a Chardonnay, I'll take that. Should I get one or two? Flying just makes me all, well, you know," she said, fluttering her hands vaguely toward her stomach.

The flight attendant offered a polite smile. "I'd suggest starting with one now, and I'll bring you the second once we're in the air."

Kathy frowned and sighed dramatically. "On second thought, I think I need two. Trust me, I've flown enough to know one just isn't going to cut it. I promise, I'll be asleep before we're even at cruising altitude."

The flight attendant hesitated but held her ground. "I understand, but I still think it's better to wait on the second. I'll even make sure it's the first thing I bring you once we're up."

Kathy waved off the advice with a dismissive gesture. "I'm good, darling. Trust me, I know what works for me. Besides, it's Wednesday. Practically the weekend, right?"

After a beat, the flight attendant gave a measured nod and said, "Yes, ma'am." She turned and walked away, and I could see her resolve shift as Kathy flashed a satisfied grin.

The boarding door closed with a final thud as the flight attendants wrapped up their safety demo and collected the last of the drinks. Kathy chugged the dregs of her wine, her hiccups making an encore just as the engines drowned them out. We taxied to the runway, and the pilot's voice crackled over the PA, apologizing for the delay and warning of some turbulence on the way up. "We'll keep the flight attendants seated for the first fifteen to twenty minutes for their safety. Flight attendants, prepare the cabin for departure."

Moments later, the final ding rang before we soared down the runway. Eight minutes after takeoff, we hit some bumps that would make even the most ardent atheist reach for some rosary beads. I heard Kathy sneeze. At least, that's what I thought it was. My seat neighbor screamed when suddenly the smell hit my nostrils. Kathy had yacked.

Kathy's seat neighbor bolted into the aisle, and she followed, gripping the headrests for support. A flight attendant quickly intercepted her: "Ma'am, please avoid touching anything until you've washed your hands."

"Definitely a seat release button moment," I thought.

Kathy stumbled toward the bathroom, leaving the flight attendants scrambling. They asked me and the guy behind me to move to empty seats while they cleaned.

Minutes later, Kathy emerged, but the flight attendant shot her down: "No, ma'am. That lavatory's your home until I say otherwise." I heard warranted applause as I headed towards the rear.

Twenty minutes later, we were allowed back. "She's out cold," the flight attendant whispered.

"Nice work. How'd you manage to knock her out?" I asked. "The bathroom door," the flight attendant said with a wink and a smile. We all trekked back to our seats.

Kathy looked as expected—disheveled and defeated, her coat draped over her like a blanket, eye mask in place. A can of club soda sat on the console beside her, and she snored softly. Fortunately, my headphones drowned out the noise, and I enjoyed the uneventfulness of the rest of the flight. Finally, we landed.

I stood up to exit the plane when Kathy bonked her head on the ceiling. "Oh, for crying out loud! Could this day get any worse?"

It could, and it did. Kathy rummaged through her tote only to realize her phone was dead. "You have to be kidding me!" she exclaimed. Then she turned to the rest of us, desperate. "Hey, pals, anyone mind ordering me an Uber? I'll Venmo you an extra twenty bucks."

No one flinched.

"Come on, now. I can't take a cab. My neighbors will call the cops," she whined, voice rising, but the collective silence said it all. No lifelines here.

I'd avoided the in-flight lavatory for obvious reasons so I dashed for the terminal restroom as soon as I deplaned. When I emerged at arrivals, there she was, frantically asking strangers how to get an Uber without a phone. They brushed past her, uninterested, while I headed toward my driver.

That's where I last saw Kathy: still solo, still stuck, and left completely on her own to figure out her next move.

As Applied in Reality

Flying Solo, Crashing Hard

Brian had the pilot and the gate agent. Samantha found the flight attendant. The Banks could've called on the club concierge, and the Whitakers really should've listened at check-in. We all need to pivot, turn smacks into lightbulb moments, and fuel ourselves for rough circumstances without becoming an asshole—but let's be real: we can't do it alone.

We need networks. Kathy had more than enough chances to accept help, take feedback, and lean on the people around her to smooth her journey. If she had, she might've made it through security in one piece—and kept the wine in her stomach instead of sharing it with the poor gal in 3A. She might've even earned some sympathy when it came time to hail an Uber—if people weren't afraid she'd stick them with a $500 vomit fine, and tank their rating with a one-star review. But no. She failed—spectacularly. The good news? We don't have to.

We all have networks—but are we really using them? And no, this doesn't mean just humbly announcing your new job on LinkedIn, "liking" others' career moves, or showing up for the occasional cocktail hour. The real question is: within your network, do you have people who will offer unsolicited help when you need it and give you the constructive feedback necessary to make important decisions? Chances are, you do. And if you're willing to accept that help and use the feedback, you can avoid a Kathy-like journey in your career—frazzled, off-course, and with far fewer allies when you need them most.

Caffeinated Assistance in the Terminal

Instead of wine, Kathy probably should've ordered a coffee. It might have led her travels down a more productive path—like, say, the one paved by the person who put that famous green siren on all our cups.

Howard Schultz didn't brew up Starbucks from scratch. While working at a coffee equipment company, it was actually his boss who suggested a trip to Italy. There, he discovered espresso bars that weren't just serving coffee—they were community hubs. That little side trip turned out to be pretty useful. From then on, Schultz made a habit of listening—whether to customers, employees, or anyone with an idea worth brewing. He didn't just build Starbucks; he built a culture where baristas weren't just pulling shots, they were calling them, too.

But Schultz's talent for building relationships didn't stop behind the counter. He forged connections with coffee suppliers and industry experts, growing Starbucks from a single Seattle shop into a global empire. It's fair to say his network and openness to advice brewed something big.

And thanks to him, I now spend $5 a day on iced coffee—fuel sources and all.

Even if we aim to emulate Schultz, we're bound to hit the same roadblocks Kathy did—that's where the rubber really meets the road.

Spilled Totes and Open Hands

My tote spilled unexpectedly the week before Christmas during my second year working with D'Andre.

That week, I flew to Miami and New York City. After months of diligence and negotiations for the two acquisitions I'd lined up, the sellers had become good friends of mine—thanks to countless hours spent together and the fact that we were all around the same age. The purpose of these trips? Prep for Day 1 transitions and to coordinate the closing celebrations. We were all set for December 31 but agreed to hold off on the festivities until after the new year. And, since most families need booze to keep holiday fights at bay, I had to make sure we'd pre-ordered enough cases of Veuve and Moët to avoid running dry.

On my flight home, I tried to use the WiFi to listen in on the board meeting. The board was supposed to rubber stamp both transactions. I just needed to hear the magic words so I could text my two friends that it was a done deal and we were officially partners. But the connection was so bad, I couldn't even send or receive iMessages. So, I ordered some bubbles, toasted myself for a job well done, and enjoyed Christmas music through my headphones the rest of the journey.

When I landed, the text messages came through.

"Doesn't look good for MIA."

"Ugh. Officially not in South Florida. Quashed."

"NYC on thin ice."

"Shit. Killed. BOTH. Unbelievable."

I called D'Andre as soon as I landed, but there was no time to commiserate. Our activist investor had convinced the board to start a "strategic alternatives review." In plain English: we weren't buying any companies—we were breaking ourselves up and selling the pieces. We had to inform the sellers. They both thought we were joking. When they realized we weren't, they went apoplectic before swearing never to talk to us again. No shit—we'd convinced them to take our offer over higher bids, put them through months of diligence, and dropped the bomb a week before the holidays. Even I wanted to throw up. The tote was fully spilled.

That night, I called Bethany. Bethany was the Director of the MBA program while I was at Ole Miss. Through my fellowship in B-school, I was selected to work directly in her office. I struck gold. Bethany evolved from my big boss to my big sister as she moved on from program director to an HR executive at a tech company. She knew my entire story and the arc of my career journey up to that point, and she still liked me. Lucky for me, she wasn't afraid to offer a helping hand—even if that meant shaking some sense into me.

"Look, you know I love you. And I know you didn't ask, but in my line of work, I have to say it—you're definitely on the chopping block. Maybe not tomorrow, but if your title involves M&A and the company's no longer pursuing that... well, you see where I'm going. Ugh. I know it was your dream job. Lick your wounds tonight, vent, pour another glass while we talk—but I'd start looking in the new year."

She'd reached down to help as the tote's contents spilled. Would I accept it? Or swat it away?

I purposely arrived at the office later than usual, hoping to catch D'Andre already there so I could read his face first. Also, I may have polished off an Oregon pinot during my call with Bethany. The tension at the office was thick, but at least we still had jobs—for today.

In January, I started my job search, and I was fortunate to land an offer quickly. D'Andre even served as a reference. I took an internal role at a consulting firm, where I'd develop and execute their go-to-market strategy for private equity. My start date? March 1, 2020. Two weeks later, the world shut down, and the guillotine came out at my former employer. D'Andre survived, but I'd have been Marie Antoinette.

Bethany's unsolicited advice was more than just a helping hand—it was a career saver. Thanks to her, I'd managed to get through security, tote in hand.

Second Pours and Opinions

By the end of my second year at the new gig. I started wondering if it was time for an additional pour—but I needed to solicit some real feedback before I tilted back the glass.

My first year in the role went down like a crisp French Sauv on a hot summer day. We reported directly to the firm's executive team, worked with practice leaders, and planned to take the message to private equity bigwigs. It was highly visible. Thanks to joining the initiative early, there was even a path to leadership.

Even better? The strategy was executed flawlessly. Revenues beat expectations in the first year, despite the COVID lockdowns. My work earned me a stellar reputation across the firm, and I even found myself in the managing director selection pool. There was just one blemish on my record.

Sure, I'd helped build the commercial strategy and the tools behind it, but I also had individual revenue goals. I missed them by, oh, I don't know, sixty percent—well within the margin of error if you're counting votes for "President" Maduro in Venezuela.

Year two was shaping up similarly. I'd developed a strong rapport with one of the firm's top practice leaders. Our friendship was built on a shared love of sarcasm and *Succession*. I'd throw fine wine in there, too, but he drinks Chardonnay. In Q2, I was asked to re-enter the selection pool, but something didn't sit right. I was a bit like Kathy, shifting uneasily in her seat.

Over dinner, I had to ask Jonathan: was the second glass really necessary? Did I really want to go through the process again if my numbers weren't trending upwards?

"I'm on track. Yeah, to replicate last year's performance," I said with a despondent smirk.

"You know, it's generally a good idea to generate enough revenue to cover your compensation, Brandon. That is, if you actually want to get promoted—or stick around," he replied, half-joking.

I laughed, tilted my head back, and shook it. "Why did I agree to this dinner?"

"For the free bottle of the Domaine Vacheron Sancerre, since you're too snooty for Chardonnay."

"I'm sorry that I don't drink wine that tastes like the teardrops in a Danielle Steel novel," I shot back.

"You're such a prick. That's why I like you. C'mon, it can't be that bad. You came here highly praised and have built a solid reputation—though I have no idea how," Jonathan teased. "Kidding, of course. So what's going on? Can't sell, or don't want to?"

I sighed. "Evidently, I'm good at strategy, building deal pipelines, and closing deals, when I have the purse—corporate development. But business development? Not my strength." I could see the wheels in Jonathan's head start to turn.

"Well, why don't we find a way for you to do that and actually make the firm some money?"

We discussed building an outsourced corporate development practice at the firm—something companies could use on an interim basis. It made sense. Many of the firm's clients were too small to justify full-time M&A teams, but they still needed help. Jonathan saw the potential immediately, and as we talked, Jonathan had clients mentally lined up, ready to test-drive the offering. It was the perfect opportunity to get my deal muscles back in action. I transferred under his wing the following week.

In the end, I didn't need that second glass of wine—I needed a new plan, a cup of coffee to steer my path more toward the Schultz way and less like Kathy. The outsourced practice idea was my way back into the M&A game. But even though I chose coffee over wine, my stomach was still unsettled. I was inching further from the dream role I'd nearly closed in on when I worked with D'Andre, and that gnawed at me. Still, I was grateful I didn't make a mess of myself—or my career. This way, at least, I could still tap my neighbors for a favor.

Passengers Willing and Able to Assist

Like Kathy, my phone battery died. If I was going to get anywhere, I'd need my fellow passengers to request an Uber. Fortunately, I was surrounded by some impressive fellow folks in the cabin.

My first go at consulting felt like a holding pattern—airborne, but just waiting for the runway lights and an exit ramp. This time? It felt more like a diversion. Maybe I wouldn't actually end up where I'd planned.

My deal muscles were certainly back in shape. Several clients test-drove the outsourced practice, and I helped them build and scale their M&A functions from scratch. It was a full-spectrum experience, and I had fun with it. I even helped two friends on the side prepare their businesses for sale. My toolkit was sharper than ever.

But there was one problem: every single client, every single deal rep—was pro bono. No revenue, zero points, and may God have mercy on my soul when review season came around. That's when the panic kicked in full throttle.

I had to suppress the sense of impending doom as I dialed into a monthly Zoom happy hour with my crew of mentees. I serve on the board for the Ole Miss MBA program, one of my roles is mentoring students—specifically, the "overdrive" types who are determined to beat the odds and break into M&A. We'd placed Matthew in my former consulting practice, where he excelled and evolved to lead private sponsors coverage at an investment bank. Kaden fought his way into a Big 4 valuation practice, then parlayed that into a bulge bracket role on Wall Street. And the newest member, Patrick, had just received an offer to work in M&A compliance for one of the largest U.S. financial institutions. We always joked that we'd outkicked our coverage—but maybe, for the first time, I actually had. After a drink, the word vomit flowed. Emphasis on *word*.

"Look man, if your utilization is that low, ouch. I know people love you there on a personal level, but they ain't no 501(c)(3). Have you seen the massive layoffs in consulting? It's coming to a theater near you if you're not billing hours. Take advantage of the love and ask folks to find you something else. Hell, if you're a client, you'll actually make them money," Matthew chimed in. "No ofende, amigo."

He wasn't wrong. When I asked the group if they had any leads—since recruiters were probably flooding their LinkedIn inboxes—Kaden perked up. "Actually, yeah. Want me to make an introduction?

Hell yes. Damn right.

The following week, I met with several colleagues-turned-friends to talk openly—but confidentially—about my predicament. They were eager to help. Naturally, it was a group of SMU and Ole Miss alums, along with a few from other schools I now try not to root against on fall Saturdays. Fittingly, it was a fellow Mustang who ended up fetching me that Uber.

Through her, I met Mark, an investment banker turned CFO. After dinner with them both, and bluntly laying out my backstory, Mark referred me for a Head of M&A role, a chance to reprise D'Andre. On paper, it was a perfect match. The industry and deal sizes mirrored my previous work, and the tools needed were exactly what I'd used on the pro bono projects at the firm to run transactions.

The interviews went smoothly—with the management team and the private equity sponsors—and then I heard that familiar line: "We'll be in touch soon."

One week. Silence. Two weeks. I followed up. They promised to get back to me by the end of the week. By Thursday, nothing. I could muster one word: "Shit." Shit, shit, shit.

Also that week, the rumor mill was swirling about layoffs at the firm. I knew I wouldn't survive the gallows. Panic set in, and I'd spiraled into full-blown doom mode. Then, after a lunch workout session on Friday, my phone rang. It was the CEO—with the offer to run M&A. It was *that* job—the one I'd heard about on that seminal call with Wayne.

Obviously I accepted. Now I just couldn't fuck it up.

The takeaway? Don't be like Kathy. How do we do that? Accept the unsolicited help. Ask for advice, seek feedback, and be willing to accept it. That pattern— the willingness to be a good seat neighbor—meant that my network, my cabin of passengers, was willing to help me get where I needed to go. You can do the same.

So, how do we know when it's time to make that final jump? Enter our last habit, the eager exiter—to remind us that rushing ahead without the right prep leaves you stumbling and won't get you there any sooner.

Chapter 8

Habit 6: The Eager Exiter

Eager Exiter (*noun*): A species notorious for their relentless desire to refute the principles of orderly disembarkation and basic decorum. Key characteristics to behold:

- Premature Risers: Swiftly rises from their seat the moment the seatbelt sign switches off at the gate, unceremoniously depositing their bags in the aisle with a devil-may-care attitude, despite being geographically lightyears away from the boarding door. Audacious claims on prime aisle real estate render it nearly impossible for anyone nearby to access bags or navigate the cramped aircraft confines.
- Verbal Vortex: Engages in a never-ending stream of self-centered banter, regaling unsuspecting victims with tales of their arduous travel day or impossibly tight connection. Believes their struggles are the stuff of legend and nobody else has ever experienced such inconveniences.
- Deplaning Dynamo: Bolts forward like a dog that notices an opening in a gate, barging past rows of patiently waiting passengers as if they hold the exclusive patent on urgency and importance.
- Delusional Dispatcher: Exhibits a perplexing belief that flight attendants and pilots possess supernatural powers to contact their next gate to hold the plane.

The Fix: You Want to ... But Probably Shouldn't

Anticipate the inevitable rush as they zoom into the aisle with their bags the moment the seatbelt sign dings off. Subtly extend your foot or shoulder into the aisle, maybe with one finger reaching up towards the overhead bin latch. As they barrel forward out of turn, click the latch so they meet your strategically placed foot, leading to an unexpected collision with the bin and a momentary halt in their tracks. As they stumble backward, act shocked and apologize profusely, claiming you were just trying to get your own bag after the row in front of you exited.

As Seen Storming the Exits

While most people are glued to their phones, scrolling through social media and comparing themselves to others, frequent flyers are busy refreshing the airline app—because let's be honest, the upgrade list is the only societal ranking that really matters.

Airlines have turned status into a metallic arms race—silver, gold, platinum, and beyond. It's no longer just about miles flown, either. The more cash you pump into the airline, the higher you climb. Add on a pricier ticket, and suddenly you're looking down on the masses like you're next in line for Prince or Princess of "Clouds." Let them eat Biscoff.

Truth be told, it's understandable. When a last-minute cross-country flight has you crammed in a middle seat, that upgrade can be the difference between arriving ready to conquer the day or crawling off the plane looking like a beaten piñata. Of course, if you score the upgrade on an evening flight home, don't plan on driving back to your bed—those friendly pours can be sneaky.

As flights get shorter, the appeal of an upgrade fades fast. On quick hops, as long as you've snagged a decent seat in premium economy, the perks are barely worth the hassle. But sometimes, even on a short flight, desperation creeps in.

One fall Sunday, I found myself in just such a bind. The weekend had been the tail end of a college football bender. It kicked off in Dallas, where I hit The Boulevard for SMU's tailgate scene—champagne flowed despite another rough loss. The football renaissance hadn't quite reached the Hilltop yet, but I was still a die-hard fan. On the flip side, Ole Miss was in a quasi-revival.

From Dallas, I flew straight back to the client site for the week. After wrapping up, I flew to Memphis and made the drive down to Oxford for round two of tailgating, this time in The Grove. Oxford was buzzing, and Ole Miss stunned Alabama in front of ESPN Gameday. More champagne flowed, and after that, things got a bit fuzzy. What I do remember clearly is the agonizing drive back to Memphis the next morning—like listening to Fergie's NBA All-Star national anthem performance on repeat for sixty-four straight minutes.

I pulled the rental car into the parking garage and caught a glimpse of myself in the rear door window. Yeah, I looked exactly like Bradley Cooper ... at around minute twenty-five of *The Hangover*. I checked the airline app as I walked toward the terminal. There was still one seat left up front, and I was number one on the upgrade list.

"Please, baby Jesus, I promise I'll never drink again."

The window wasn't normally my preferred seat, but today I could rest my throbbing head against the wall. And besides, it was a thirty-eight-minute flight—I was so dehydrated, I didn't have to worry about asking someone to get up to use the restroom. The only thing I'd be passing was a kidney stone.

I rode up the escalator toward security, head still pounding. At the top, I braced myself for a quick step off, but the TSA line had snaked so far back it was blocking the exit. Passengers were doing that awkward shuffle, trying to avoid a pile-up without leaving enough space for anyone to slip through. It was Sunday morning, and a drawn-out TSA ordeal was not on my bingo card.

Fortunately, the PreCheck line was wide open, barely past the first stanchion. I dodged my way over, flashed my boarding pass, and that's where I encountered Grayson.

Despite my headphones being in, I could still sense Grayson—mainly because he was practically breathing down my neck. He was so close that when he tapped his foot, it rattled my bag. The airport was crowded, so I ignored it. But when the line inched forward and he bumped into me, I couldn't ignore that.

Finally, he tapped me on the shoulder. "Hi. My wife's already at the gate, and she's waiting on me if you don't mind," he explained, flustered.

I wasn't in a hurry and definitely wasn't looking to chat, so I waved him through. He moved ahead, using the same rushed excuse on everyone else. Despite his frantic pace, he only managed to cut off two or three people, shaving maybe a couple of minutes off his time.

By the time we reached the security check, though, his flustered routine caught up with him. In his rush to get through, he forgot to take the electronics out of his pocket, setting off the detectors. Ironically, we wound up clearing security at the same time.

Once I collected my belongings, I made a beeline for the SkyClub. It was an unusually quiet lounge—low traffic with dim lighting, and a perfect corner seat open with no neighbors. After pouring some coffee and grabbing a banana, I checked the upgrade list. Still number one. Still one seat left.

The inbound plane landed, so I chugged some water and headed towards the gate. Ugh. It was Sunday. The concourse would be crawling with "leisure travelers." Getting to the gate on weekends felt like playing a real-life game of *Frogger*.

During the week, travelers had purpose, especially in the mornings and late afternoons. That purpose disappeared on weekends unless it was to enrage the regulars. Families would park themselves in the middle of the concourse, kids doing cartwheels as if it were their personal playground. Then there's the guy who cuts you off, only to stop dead right in front of you, completely oblivious. But the worst? The wall of friends walking four-wide, arms outstretched, dragging their wheeled bags beside them like an impenetrable barrier.

I weaved and ducked through the crowd to the gate. As I dodged the deplaning passengers, I heard the gate agent butcher my last name over the PA system. Upgrade cleared. Score. Time to grab my new boarding pass for 4A.

Lo and behold, I found myself in line behind Grayson, who was standing at the podium with his wife. He gave off total dad vibes—chinos, a tucked-in polo with no belt, and blindingly white tennis shoes. His wife clung to her cardigan like it was a security blanket.

Apparently, Grayson had tried to get cute with their reservation. He booked his wife in first class, hoping he'd snag an upgrade himself and convince someone to switch seats. She wasn't a fan of flying and wanted to sit next to him. Problem was, he was number two on the upgrade list, and the last seat? Well, that went to me.

They both walked away, defeated. Given the circumstances, I was hoping the gate agent might quietly slip me my new boarding pass, letting me avoid their wrath. Naturally, she used her outside voice, announcing my upgrade loud enough for the entire terminal to hear.

Instead of the heavy breathing at security, now I could practically feel Grayson's glares burning through me. Luckily, his wife needed to use the restroom, and he went off to show her the way, ending the standoff.

As soon as they disappeared, boarding began, and I made my way onto the MD-88. I sort of miss those birds—especially the PA system that made flight attendants sound like the teacher from *Peanuts* on a good day.

I took my seat in row 4, the last row of first class. About ten minutes later, Grayson and his wife appeared. Naturally, she was my new aisle seat neighbor, while Grayson was seated directly behind us in the first row of premium economy.

As the plane started to fill up, she kept nervously glancing at the empty seats up front, whispering to Grayson about whether one might open up for him. You could see her anxiety ramping up as each seat was claimed, her hope fading with every passenger who boarded.

I turned up the volume on my headphones, shut the window shade, and closed my eyes, trying to stave off the inevitable "hangxiety" that was creeping in thanks to their running commentary. The slow trickle of boarding passengers finally stopped, and every last seat in first class had been snapped up. Suddenly, I felt a tap.

She gestured toward the window. "Could you open the shade? It helps my nerves."

"Really?" I thought, but obliged without taking out my headphones. Maybe that would be the end of it.

Tap. Again.

This time, she wanted me to take out my headphones. "Do you know how to open the tray table? I like to be prepared for once we're in the air."

Great.

What followed was a barrage of questions. "Was I going home or was Memphis home? Do you fly this route often? How long is the flight? Have you ever hit turbulence on this leg?"

Despite my best efforts to look unwelcoming—hat, headphones, the whole nine yards—her nervous energy was relentless. Bright lights, chatty neighbor? Fuck this.

I took a deep breath and turned to her. "Would you like me to switch seats with your husband?"

Grayson was practically in my lap before I could finish the question. The flight attendant, clearly noticing my annoyance, stepped in. "Sir, you'll need to let him out first if you're switching seats."

He nodded eagerly, and his wife quickly shuffled into the window seat as he took the aisle. But, of course, the ordeal wasn't over. Grayson then spent the next five minutes with the flight attendants, rearranging bags in the overhead compartment so he could move his a whopping one row forward.

I took my new seat when my neighbor poked me. "Wait—weren't you the one doing the Macarena on the jumbotron at the game yesterday?!"

"I don't know that person," I deadpanned.

She laughed and patted my arm. "Yeah, you probably need some sleep, darling."

The flight itself was blissfully uneventful. We landed twenty minutes ahead of schedule and started our taxi to the gate—my word, there was even an open gate.

The plane stopped just short of the gate, and I saw Grayson inching upward. "He's one of those," I thought.

Right on cue, the flight attendant's voice crackled over the PA. I could just make out Charlie Brown's teacher's words over the usual feedback: "Ladies and gentlemen, we are just shy of the gate. Please stay seated until the captain has turned off the seat belt sign."

Seconds later, the plane rolled forward into its parking spot, the brakes gently rocking the cabin.

Ding.

It was like a starter pistol went off. Passengers bolted from their seats, jostling for position in the cramped aisle. The first row made sense—they had a clear path to freedom. The second? Maybe, if the first row had already bulldozed into the galley. But everyone else? It was pure madness. People twisted and contorted, yanking bags from overhead bins, trying to wedge themselves into spaces that didn't exist. The whole thing felt like a cross between musical chairs and Twister, minus the fun. All to save maybe twenty seconds.

And then there was Grayson—leading the charge. He shot up like he'd been catapulted, frantically yanking both his and his wife's bags from the overhead bin. His suitcase tipped over in the aisle, and he kept handing his wife the wrong purse. After a few tries, he finally located the correct Dooney & Bourke while the passengers behind him shifted awkwardly, waiting for the human traffic jam to clear.

Finally, Grayson managed to get his roller bag upright and began pushing it down the aisle, bumping into seatbacks along the way, each impact slowing him down. When he eventually reached the door, I glanced at the passengers in my row. We were right behind him, stepping into the terminal mere nanoseconds after his much-anticipated exit.

As Applied in Reality

A Rushed Journey

Building a network that helps you navigate the ups and downs takes time. Sometimes, there just aren't any shortcuts—you've got to embrace the process. Take Grayson, he rushed through security and landed a seat toward the front of the plane, only to end up arriving inside the terminal at the same time as everyone else.

Now, I'm not here to tell you to "wait your turn"—though on a plane, that's solid advice. And I'm definitely not here to say entrepreneurs shouldn't go after what they want, or that office politics don't play a part in the promotion Olympics. What I'm saying is this: if you focus on gaining experience while you're in your own seat, you'll be ready to make your move when the opportunity comes. Force it before you're ready, and you risk fumbling your ascent—right in front of a plane full of people ready to trample you on the way out.

If Grayson flipped through SiriusXM stations the way he rushed through the airport, he probably missed a certain podcaster's show. And when it came to her journey, she took a very different approach—one that appreciated the long haul and positioned her perfectly to make her move.

In Due Time

Regardless of your opinion on her politics, there's no denying that Megyn Kelly is a force in the media. She's one of the top podcasters in America now, but she didn't get there overnight. Megyn earned that audience through major stints at two of the country's biggest news organizations.

She didn't exactly take the express lane there, either. She went to law school at Albany—not quite the Ivy League—and fought hard to land her first job. Her "upgrade" came when she made the move to prestigious Jones Day, a top-tier law firm. She practiced for several years before she took a severe pay cut for a career change in a new arena: news. Despite her law firm background, she had to start local. But here's the thing—she doesn't regret that long journey. In fact, her time as a lawyer is what gave her the credibility and expertise that made her stand out when she transitioned to media. That legal background became her edge, helping her rise through the ranks and eventually land in the national spotlight. Her experiences with the major networks are what propelled and positioned her to run her own show independently.

Even when it seemed like an upgrade might not happen, Megyn focused on her experiences. She was prepared and ready to step into her next role when the time came, proving that sometimes, the long road gives you exactly what you need to succeed.

Security Lines Shaping the Journey

First, we have to learn to appreciate the journey. It's not always easy.

That Sunday, Grayson blitzed through the security line, all impatience and agitation, trying to muscle his way ahead of the process. Spoiler alert: it didn't work. How often do we pull that move in our careers? How many times do we try to fast-forward the process that Megyn Kelly endured?

I get it. You're probably thinking, "Man, you could've been the Head of M&A way sooner if you'd skipped law school, jumped straight into consulting or banking, and grabbed an MBA." Trust me, I used to have that thought on repeat—therapy wasn't cheap. But here's the thing: yeah, I might've shaved off a few years, but would I be the same person, the same professional without all these experiences? And if not, would I have been as prepared for the role?

When I stepped into the dream gig, our private equity sponsors and the executive team threw me straight into the deep end—sink or swim. Honestly, I wouldn't have had it any other way. I walked into a deal that was practically on life support. The seller had deal fatigue so bad, he handed over all transaction duties to his wife just so he could focus on running the business. Meanwhile, the lawyers, CPAs, and advisors were at each other's throats. During my first meeting, the morale was so low, I half-expected one of those creepy deep-sea fish to float by. And, in parallel, I had to build rapport and respect within my own team, who were probably thinking, "Who the hell is this new guy, and why is he telling us what to do?" A month later, we closed the deal.

I'm no miracle worker. I like what I do, and I'd like to think I'm pretty good at it, but it was the wait in the metaphorical TSA line that really brought it all together. D'Andre instilled in me a genuine respect for founders, which helped me build trust with sellers—even if they weren't fans of my hair products or four-way stretch pants. My tax background broke down walls with the CPAs, and having a law degree meant the lawyers spoke to me, not at me, as we wrapped up negotiations. Consulting taught me how to quickly build and deploy a team to set us all up for success, and how to keep the deal on track and organized. It was the sum of those experiences that gave our sponsors and CEO the confidence I'd get the job done. Most importantly, it was the setbacks and hard-earned lessons from my own journey that gave me the credibility to look the seller in the eye and say, "Don't worry. We're going to close this," even when they couldn't see the light at the end of the tunnel.

In just over a year, we acquired eleven businesses. We closed every deal once we executed the LOI. I don't want to jinx it, but with our perfect batting average, the team might be headed for a first-round ballot induction into the Hall of Fame. I'd give you their names, but I need recruiters to stay out of their LinkedIn mailboxes, at least for a few more years. Together, we've planted flags in four new states and eight new markets. We've also made a lot of new friends. And honestly, the fun's just getting started.

The journey itself was kind of fun—in retrospect, of course. There's a lot to be grateful for, and looking back, I can see why each step mattered. SMU let me dream big, and those dreams led me to South Carolina. There, I met Professors Lad and Brant, discovered tax, and landed my first job at the launch pad. Ole Miss brought me Wayne, and listening in on one of his calls, I finally realized what I wanted to be when I grew up.

It wasn't just about career moves as I grew up, though. Thanks to law school, I introduced my childhood best friend to his wife. Law school and business school took me to Atlanta, where I found a decade-long support system and lifelong friends like Reid. I even got to witness Reid's daughter strap on her first pair of skis. Reid introduced me to Wayne, who not only became a mentor but also brought me into a "band of brothers" in Oxford—a crew so tight it felt like we'd known each other since kindergarten. And, of course, SMU gave me Amanda, my lifelong friend who wouldn't let me stop writing after school—so, yes, you can blame her for making you read all these pages. The people I met at every stop supported both my professional and personal development that was critical to my success.

Each person in that TSA line was like a checkpoint—a moment that slowed things down but shaped the journey. Grayson seemed intent on rushing past it all to get to the same destination, but I'm glad I took Megyn Kelly's path, even if my audience is just slightly smaller. Yeah, just a smidge.

Upgrade and Out

And so we come to our final point. As we learn to appreciate the journey, it's not just about the title—it's about the experience we gain and how we use it. Because, let's face it, if you score an upgrade without knowing how to make the most of the seat, you'll still end up in the same place as everyone else. Maybe just with a slightly fancier view—and in Grayson's case, that view only lasted for thirty-eight minutes.

I took a similar spill at the exit right before B-school graduation. During our spring semester, a group of us developed a pitch for what is now basically JSX or Aero—a small, hybrid-commercial airline that bypasses TSA. Yes, I was trying to avoid strangers on airplanes long before I'd even earned my first airline status.

We were through the roof about the project after we'd earned a trip to Dallas to pitch the idea to a few folks at Southwest Airlines. We had it all worked out—divvied up the C-suite seats, and I was CEO, of course. We were certain they'd hire us on the spot to make it happen. But here's the thing—just like Grayson, we weren't quite ready. That's being generous. Thankfully so were they. Our audience politely shredded the model, crushed our dreams, and pointed out we hadn't raised the $375 million in capital we needed to start, let alone used the right industry KPIs in our analysis. Oops.

We left that pitch bruised but not broken. On the drive back, our crew dissected everything we didn't know yet—what it would really take to run a business of that scale. The more we talked, the more obvious it became that we had a lot of learning and growing to do before we could even think about making something like that happen. But that realization planted a seed—it helped me understand that while ambition is great, it's the experience gained along the way that truly prepares you for the role, not just the fancy title.

In the rat race, that lesson came in handy—especially in professional services, where it's so easy to get wrapped up in titles and promotions. You want the first-class seat. You want to humbly announce to the LinkedIn "community" that you're "honored to start a new role." You don't want your peers deplaning before you. But let's be honest—how many times have you seen someone politic their way to a title, only to fumble the deplaning process like Grayson?

Every time I didn't get a promotion, I had to admit—deep down—it wasn't totally undeserved. Yeah, it stung, but if I'm being honest, there was more for me to learn (and therapy to schedule). Those moments always seemed to come at critical times, too. Megyn Kelly faced her own obstacles, and while the stakes were just slightly higher for her, the pattern was familiar. When she left her evening news gig at one network, she pivoted to a morning show for more family time. When that stint wrapped up, she decided to be her own boss—and, spoiler alert, she made it happen. The exits probably stung a bit, but they gave her the experience she needed to go solo.

My missed promotions? Same story, minus anybody knowing or caring. Sure, unlike Kelly, I had to accept that my skill set wasn't quite there yet (tax) or that I was a bit too laser-focused in one area (consulting). But honestly, those rejections kept me focused on the long game, forcing me to gain the experience I needed. In the end, it wasn't the title I needed—it was the growth to actually handle the role I wanted.

But wait—wasn't I supposed to be a sports agent? Didn't I want to be the next *Jerry Maguire*? I said it worked out, right? So... how did that happen?

My day job? Well, it's not exactly "sports agent to the stars," but it hits many of the same notes. No, I'm not negotiating multimillion-dollar contracts for athletes. Instead, I'm scouting for talent—but in the business world. I spend my time getting to know owners, learning about their vision, culture, and whether they'd be a fit with our enterprise. Think of it like matching an athlete with the perfect endorsement deal—just without the locker room drama. Once we're aligned, it's all about closing the deal. High stakes? Check. Adrenaline rush? Absolutely. And sellers are a lot easier to deal with than professional athletes—I've yet to receive a 3:00 a.m. call to post bail after a nightclub brawl.

And while the *Jerry Maguire* dream took on a new shape, it became something even more rewarding through my involvement with SMU's *Life After Ball* program. The program helps student-athletes who aren't heading to the pros make the leap from the field to the professional world—a jump that can feel like going from center stage to the back row in coach. These athletes have spent their lives focused on sports, and when that chapter closes, the next step isn't always clear. That's where we step in.

We mentor them, introduce them to career opportunities, and help them get their careers in flight (minus the TSA lines). We're not just "showing them the money," we're helping them figure out how to bring their game off the field and into the boardroom. Watching them transition with the same intensity and drive they had on the field is incredible—honestly, it's one of the most rewarding things I've been a part of.

And the best part? This entire journey—mentoring athletes, scouting businesses, closing deals—started right at SMU. That's where the dream began, and it's where it came full circle.

So, what's the takeaway here? It's simple—the upgrade or title is just a starting position. The real journey is in the experience you gain along the way, and the wisdom you collect from every delay, fumble, and missed opportunity. Whether you're Grayson racing to the front of the plane only to realize you've arrived at the same place, or a business school grad watching your million-dollar pitch unravel, the lesson remains: it's not about how fast you get there—it's about being ready when you do. And as I've learned, it's often the long, winding path that prepares you for the moments that matter most. It's best to enjoy the ride.

So just like that, we've come to the exit. You've made it. It's your turn to deplane the aircraft. Now grab your bags, and don't be an asshole—move with purpose and don't hold up the rest of us.

Chapter 9

Final Destination?

I didn't become Jeff Bezos, Mr. Wonderful, or Bill Ackman, much less Drew Rosenhaus or Leigh Steinberg. If you're disappointed, welcome to my family's Thanksgiving dinner. Trust me, you're in good company. I get it. We haven't exactly cracked the code to solving life's major problems in these pages, but if you've laughed, cringed, or even nodded along, I'd say we've landed the plane and brought it to the gate safely. And honestly, learning to laugh at the turbulence was what kept me from bailing out mid-flight. At the very least, I hope you've picked up a few survival tricks for navigating both the literal and professional skies.

You've probably noticed that none of these chapters handed you a foolproof way to avoid strange behaviors. Well, nothing approved by the FAA, anyway. Instead, we focused on addressing the chaos and finding ways to deal with it—sometimes with patience, often with sarcasm. Why? Because avoiding these behaviors starts with us. If we want the madness to end—whether it's at the airport or in the office—we have to make sure we're not the ones fueling it. And, like with anything else, that takes practice. Lots of reps. Muscle memory.

Now, about those reps. Sure, I've talked about fitness as a fuel source, but here's my confession: I hate running. Despise it. If you ever see me running outside, do yourself a favor and run faster—because either a bear or a cop is chasing me. But, like it or not, cardio is necessary. Enter TJ and Training Mate. With their circuit training, banter, and killer playlists, I manage to get my cardio in without feeling like I'm being hunted. The structure is there, but it's never boring. And even on the days when stress has me dragging, I show up because I know TJ will get my ass in gear. I've never left a class thinking, "Well, that was a waste of time."

Just like TJ gets me moving in the gym, we all need someone—or something—pushing us outside of it too. Whether it's in our careers or while navigating life's unpredictable flights, we need those "reps." Because, like fitness, travel and career development are ongoing. There's no finish line.

There's Always Another Flight

The good news? The lessons we've covered here? They're solid exercises for your professional muscles. The bad news? You've got to be your own TJ. No one's going to do the heavy lifting for you, but trust me, putting these lessons into practice will keep your career—and your sanity—in good shape.

Now, let's circle back to the very beginning: Susan and Steve. They collided at the departures area, but they eventually made it to Philadelphia, albeit on a later flight. If they'd bothered to turn around at the gate after deplaning, they'd have seen their plane already being prepped for its next flight. If they'd checked their apps, they'd have seen a return flight waiting—and maybe even another segment beyond that.

Their journey wasn't over; it was just one of many stops along the way.

And I'd bet Steve learned to look up from his phone as he walked through the airport, instead of rating his Uber driver a one-star rating for missing the drop-off point. As for Susan? Maybe she rethought sprinting in her Tory Burch flats and realized it's okay to pace yourself. They took those experiences, adjusted, and handled the next flight differently because of what they learned.

We've got to approach our professional journeys the same way. Where you are today? It's probably not your final stop. Whether you're loving every minute or itching to write a resignation letter as brilliant and scathing as Bill Keenan's, odds are you'll find yourself in a new role with new people and a fresh set of challenges before long. If we want to keep leveling up, we need those "workouts"—we've got to treat every experience as a chance to learn, adapt, and improve.

If we do that, we'll know exactly when to take off, when to climb and level, and when to follow the runway lights to land the plane.

So here we are. The end of the line—or at least the end of this flight. I know you had a choice in your literary travels. Thanks for flying with me.

"Tonight, most people will be welcomed home by jumping dogs and squealing kids and thousands more will ask about their day and tonight they'll sleep. The stars will wheel forth from their daytime hiding places; and one of those lights, slightly brighter than the rest, will be my wingtip passing over." – Ryan Bingham, Up in Air (2009)

As you continue your journey, whether it's through airport terminals or the winding paths of your career, I invite you to join me on this flight. Let's navigate these skies together. Download your safety information card at www.brandonblewett.com to be prepared for whatever comes your way.

Don't miss out—scan the QR code now and see where it takes you!

Dedication and Acknowledgments

Just as pilots, flight attendants, gate agents, reservation agents, and baggage handlers are the unsung heroes who guide us through the skies, my journey has been shaped by those who've helped me navigate the ups and downs of this journey. They've offered refreshment when I needed a boost, words of encouragement when I was grounded, and, yes, even the occasional warning when I headed straight toward significant turbulence.

To those who've supported me, uplifted me, challenged me, and kept me on course—thank you. You rightly didn't endorse every maneuver, but you were always an important part of the journey. And after all, what's a flight without a few bumps along the way?

Thank you for being my heroes, whether you handed me a metaphorical cocktail or a much-needed reality check. Wheels up, and cheers!

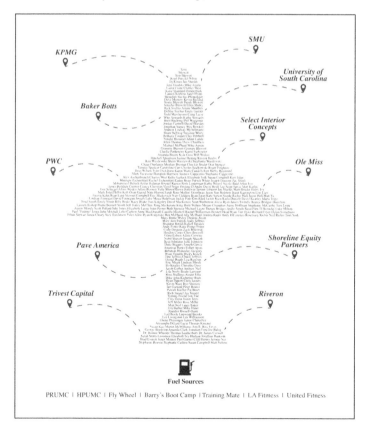